BLACK ✦ STARS

AFRICAN HEROES

JIM HASKINS

WILEY

John Wiley & Sons, Inc.

Published by John Wiley & Sons, Inc., Hoboken, New Jersey
Published simultaneously in Canada

Design and composition by Navta Associates, Inc.

For general information about our other products and services, please contact our Customer Care Department within the United States at (800) 762-2974, outside the United States at (317) 572-3993 or fax (317) 572-4002.

Wiley also publishes its books in a variety of electronic formats. Some content that appears in print may not be available in electronic books. For more information about Wiley products, visit our web site at www.wiley.com.

Library of Congress Cataloging-in-Publication Data:
Haskins, James, date.
   African heroes / Jim Haskins.
         p. cm.
   Includes bibliographical references and index.
   ISBN 0-471-46672-7
1. Africa—Biography. 2. Heroes—Africa—Biography. I. Title.
   DT18.H37 2005
   920.06—dc22

                                                                    2004014899

Printed in the United States of America
10 9 8 7 6 5 4 3 2 1

CONTENTS

INTRODUCTION

✦

Africa is a huge and diverse continent. Its geography features vast arid deserts, including the Sahara, the largest desert in the world. Africa also has fertile green valleys watered by sparkling rivers, including the longest river in the world, the Nile. Its people are equally diverse. In fact, there are more ethnic groups in Africa than in any other place on earth.

By around 5000 BC, the peoples of Africa had organized into communities of farmers and herders who engaged in commerce with one another and who shared similar beliefs in the powers of natural things and of ancestors. Some of those societies became highly developed long before the ancient European empires of Greece and Rome came into being. The ancient African empires that preceded them also had heroic figures whose charisma, bravery, and leadership abilities were legendary.

Around 1000 BC, Arab traders began to cross the vast Sahara, bringing with them not only goods but also their Muslim faith. Many Africans who came into contact with the Arabs converted to Islam and adopted that religion's belief in one all-powerful God, although some also retained aspects of their pre-Islam faith such as the power of natural phenomena. A number of African Islamic societies also became highly developed civilizations and produced their own heroes.

Europeans began to arrive in the 1400s, seeking trade routes to India. Their search led them to discover the treasures of Africa, which included spices, gold, and ivory. The Europeans established trade agreements with various African rulers.

Slavery had long existed in Africa, and the slave trade was a major part of commerce with the Arabs. Slaves were not restricted to hard labor and sometimes held positions of great responsibility. Slaves usually had rights and were recognized as human beings. After the discovery of the Americas, however, the slave trade took on a whole new aspect as millions of Africans were captured and shipped off to work in South America, the Caribbean, and North America, where they had no rights and were treated as property. Many Africans did not realize that by continuing to fight and conquer one another in order to win slaves, they were paving the way for the European takeover of their lands. The slave trade's peak years, 1740 to 1810, saw the splintering and merging of ethnic groups and the breakdown of societies. In this weakened state, Africa was ripe for conquest.

In the 1800s and early 1900s, several European nations established colonies in Africa and imposed their faith, Christianity. Many African leaders fought valiantly against European domination. Only one succeeded: Menelik II of Ethiopia, who you'll read about in this book. The borders of the African colonies created by France, Great Britain, Holland, Spain, Belgium, Germany, and Italy did not coincide with the boundaries that divided the native ethnic groups. Subjugated by outsiders, some native Africans lost their traditions and their sense of identity. Others, however, found ways to accommodate to the new systems and to work within them to help their people. Their stories can also be found within.

After World War II, a number of heroic men and women in several African countries led movements against European colonial rule. Beginning in 1957, the success of those independence movements changed the political nature of Africa. Gold Coast became independent from Great Britain and took the name Ghana in that year. Three years later, Nigeria also won independence, and the former Belgian Congo became independent Zaire. In 1961, Sierra Leone won its independence from Britain. By 1963, there were thirty-two independent African nations, representatives of which met in Addis Ababa, Ethiopia, to form the Organization of African Unity. The OAU's primary aim was to "decolonize" the remaining bastions of white rule in Southern Rhodesia, South Africa, Mozambique, and Angola. The holdouts were successful for three more decades, but even they eventually succumbed to the sea change in African political affairs.

A few new African nations managed to thrive, but many did not. Their natural resources had been depleted during colonization, and their human resources had been similarly diminished. Within the same borders created by the European colonialists, newly independent countries fell prey to interethnic rivalries. But today's Africa also has positive, visionary leaders whose example may influence other leaders as they struggle to make their nations self-sustaining and prosperous.

The names of the men and women who are profiled in these pages are both well known and little known. The facts of their lives are well documented in historical records as well as in oral history and legend. Some heroes were strong and conquering; others were quiet and peaceable. Most, being human, had weaknesses and did not always act in heroic ways, but each displayed the qualities of leadership, courage, and imagination that made them heroes of Africa.

PART ONE

◆

Heroes of Ancient and Medieval Africa

IMHOTEP

(c. 2980 BC)

Five thousand years ago, Egypt, in North Africa, was divided into two parts, now usually called Lower Egypt and Upper Egypt. Around that time, Egypt emerged as one nation, united under the single rule of a divine king. Imhotep was the ruler of what we now call the Old Kingdom. He was born a commoner, and his father was an architect named Kanofer and his mother was named Khreduonkh. Like other ancient Egyptians, Imhotep was dark skinned.

Nothing is known about his education or training, but he was a remarkable man with extensive skills and knowledge in many fields, and he was a prominent member of the royal courts of four different kings. Imhotep was an architect, like his father. In fact, he is best known today as the chief architect of the Step Pyramid at Saqqara, the oldest pyramid and one of the architectural wonders of the ancient world. He designed this pyramid for King Zoser (or Djoser) of Egypt's Third Dynasty. As a poet and philosopher, Imhotep's sayings have survived to this day, such as "Eat, drink, and be merry, for tomorrow we shall die." He was an advisor and scribe to the king and the author of many texts.

Imhotep was also a magician, a priest, an astronomer, and the chief doctor to the king in an era when all four areas of endeavor were closely allied. The Egyptians had very advanced knowledge of medicine in Imhotep's time. They understood the principles of blood circulation four thousand years before they were known in Europe. They knew how to diagnose more than two hundred diseases, practiced surgery, and made medicines from plants. Imhotep was an especially skilled physician, and after his death legends grew about him. By around 500 BC his fame had grown to such an extent that he was worshiped as a kind of god of medicine.

During the rise of the ancient Greek civilization Imhotep's influence was significant in the development of Greek medicine. The same was true in ancient Rome, where the emperors Claudius and Tiberius had inscriptions praising Imhotep on the walls of their temples. The early Roman Christians depicted him as a healer, a giver of rest, and a prince of peace.

The great temple of Amen at Karnak contains two relief sculptures of Imhotep, and a temple was built in his honor on an island in the Nile called Philae. Although the Greek physician Hippocrates is generally regarded as the father of modern medicine, in actuality the Egyptian Imhotep should be given that honor.

PIANKHY

(c. 720 BC)

The land immediately to the south of Egypt that is now part of Ethiopia was once called Nubia. Arab traders gave it that name because it was rich in gold (*nub* means gold in Arabic). Below Nubia was the kingdom of Kush, named for a very old civilization. Both of these areas were under the domination of Egypt for nearly two thousand years. Not only did they pay tribute to Egypt in gold, they also provided Egypt's kings and queens with their best fighting men. In the eighth century BC, Piankhy, King of Nubia, decided he'd had enough of Egyptian domination and he used Nubia's gold and warriors to conquer Egypt.

Piankhy was the son of King Kashta and his wife Pebatma. As was often the custom among royal families, he married his sister Peksater and had four other wives. By all accounts, he preferred peace and avoided military activity whenever possible. But when he came to the throne in 744 BC, the power of Egypt, the world's greatest nation at the time, had splintered, and he took the opportunity that presented itself.

Piankhy laid careful plans. He ordered the outfitting of a large fleet to carry his army and its supplies. Then, in a procession that stretched for miles, he started up the Nile River. Entering Egypt, he ordered that all the small towns along the river be attacked and conquered. When the fleet reached the fortress at Hermopolis, Piankhy's forces laid siege to this important city, and its ruler surrendered himself and his treasury. The fleet then continued up the Nile, capturing cities and towns along the way until it came to Memphis. This great city was surrounded by high walls and had a large fighting force and abundant supplies. Pianky was surprised at the strength of the city's defenses, but he devised a clever plan to capture it. Avoiding the walls that protected the west side of the city, he ordered his forces to the east. This side was also protected by walls, but they were not as high because of the natural protection of the river. Piankhy's fleet attacked the ships in the harbor, then lined those ships plus his own against the east walls of the city so that his men could use them as a staging area for their assault on the east walls. Soon Memphis was also under his control.

Piankhy next headed for Heliopolis, where all of the surrounding kings surrendered without resistance. Piankhy broke through the bolts and opened the doors of Egypt's holiest temple to the great sun god Amen-Ra. He then sealed them with his own seal as a symbol of his mastery of Egypt. Later, he ordered a huge granite slab produced for the temple. Inscribed on the four sides of the slab was the story of his conquering expedition. He also ordered many new temples constructed, to establish for history that he was a great conqueror. By the time Piankhy headed back home, the ships of his fleet were heavy with silver, gold, and copper.

Piankhy reigned over much of Egypt for about thirty-one years. In 712 BC, he was succeeded by his brother Sabacon who conquered additional territory in Assyria and Palestine and became king of a unified Egypt. One of Piankhy's sons, Taharka, later held the throne. After about a century, however, Nubian power waned as new conquerors arose. Piankhy was largely forgotten. The stone slab on which his victory was recounted has survived, however. It was discovered in 1862 in the ruins of the temple of Amen-Ra at Nepata, the capital of Nubia. Inscribed on all four sides with lines of hieroglyphics, it excited historians and led to a rediscovery of Piankhy. The slab, now called the Victory Stela, is currently held by the Cairo Museum in Egypt.

YOUSSEF I

(1007–1108)

By about AD 900, Arab traders had reached the region of Africa south of the Sahara Desert. The Sahara is so vast that the Arabs likened it to a sea, and the word they used for the land south of the desert was Sahel, their word for shore.

In ancient times there must have been as many heroes in this part of Africa as there were in Egypt and Ethiopia to the east, but the lack of a written language in the region prevents us from knowing about them. Not until the Arabs began writing about Africa south of the Sahara do we get written historical records about the Sahel.

The first great kingdom of the Sahel was Ghana in West Africa. In spite of its name, it has little relationship to the modern nation of Ghana. Ancient Ghana encompassed what is now northern Senegal and southern Mauritania, about four hundred miles northwest of modern Ghana. Around AD 1000 it established its influence as a center for the iron industry, then rose to great power through the gold trade with Arabs from North Africa, reaching its height of power and influence in the eleventh century. But the rise of the Almoravids to the north eventually splintered the kingdom of Ghana.

The Almoravids were an Islamic sect that originated in the desert north of Ghana in what became Upper Senegal in French West Africa. They were part of the nomadic Berber-speaking people, regarded as the indigenous tribes of North Africa, who had been converted to Islam by Arab traders. Yahyaa ibn Ibrahim, a sultan or chieftain of this group, went on a pilgrimage to Mecca (at least once in a lifetime, Muslims must travel to Mecca, in present-day Saudi Arabia, to pray at the Ka'aba, the most holy site of Islam). He returned about 1040 with ideas that he later translated into a new religious sect, the Almoravids. This new version of Islam was marked by strict obedience to the Muslim holy book, the Qur'an, and punishment of every breach of religious law, even by chiefs. Within fifteen years of Yahya's return from Mecca, the Almoravids had begun to impose their strict interpretations of the faith upon the other Berber tribes of the desert.

These fervent Muslims declared holy war against the kingdom of Ghana, which was already unstable politically. For at least two centuries, the spread of the Sahara Desert, the overuse of arable land, and the growing influence of Islam had threatened the kingdom's unity. The Almoravid invasion of 1076 pushed Ghana over the edge, weakening the empire so much that it finally collapsed altogether as individual tribal groups and chieftaincies seceded and declared their independence.

A high-ranking commander under Yahya was Youssef ben Tachfin, a member of the Masufah tribe on the northern border of the Sudan. He was of medium build with a soft voice and a strong personality. He also had dreams of power. When Yahya's first-in-command and successor, Abu Bekr, departed on an expedition to Tunis, he left Youssef in charge. Abu Bekr's trust was misplaced, however, for as soon as he was gone Youssef set about winning power for himself. He persuaded the chief priests to proclaim him ruler of the Almoravids and in 1070 ordered the construction of a capital city for his kingdom. That city, Marrakesh, is still the capital of Morocco.

By the time Abu Bekr returned from Tunis, Youssef had so completely displaced him that he didn't even try to regain his power and retired to the Sudan after being wounded by a poisoned arrow in a battle with local non-Muslim Negroes.

Youssef began to conquer more territory, and eventually his empire was larger than Western Europe. So powerful was his Islamic empire that the Moors (the Muslim rulers of Spain) asked Youssef for help in holding onto their empire.

In the eighth century, the Moors had crossed the Strait of Gibraltar, defeated the Goths, and became rulers of Spain. They later crossed the Pyrenees Mountains and conquered southern France. In the tenth century, however, the Christians of the Iberian Peninsula had defeated the Moors in southern France and pushed them back into Spain. The Moors appealed to Youssef to help them hold on to the territory they still controlled, chiefly in cities in the east and west such as Seville and Granada.

Youssef was almost eighty years old, but he did not hesitate to answer the Moors' call for help. He crossed the Strait of Gibraltar with a Muslim army of fifteen thousand men, his best fighters, among whom were six thousand Senegalese mounted on white Arabian warhorses. On the other side, Alphonso VI of Spain led seventy thousand Christian warriors, including thousands of French knights in full armor.

The two armies engaged in combat at Zalacca in October 1086. At first it seemed that there would be no contest, because the Christian forces were much larger and better equipped than those of the Moors and the Almoravids. Youssef wished he had brought more men with him. Pretending to have power he did not have, he boldly sent a messenger to Alphonso, offering him a choice of when to begin the conflict. Alphonso responded that as the next day, Friday, was the Muslim holy day, Saturday was that of the Jews, and Sunday was that of the Christians, they would do battle on Monday.

But Alphonso had chosen Monday as a trick. On Friday, as Youssef went to pray, the Christian forces attacked. Youssef then decided to play a trick of his own. While some of his forces battled those of Alphonso, another force sneaked up behind the Christian encampment and set fire to the soldiers' tents. Crowded into a narrow space between attacking Muslim forces, the great numbers of Alphonso's forces were at a disadvantage. Frightened by the fires, their horses bolted. Half of Alphonso's men were killed, and only nightfall permitted a wounded Alphonso to escape with about one hundred and fifty men. But Alphonso's forces rallied and beat back Youssef's forces. He finally withdrew and returned to his own kingdom.

For three years, Youssef refused further requests to aid the Moors in Spain, although he fully intended to return and to take power there. When he finally accepted the Moors' appeals, he went with a huge force that engaged in five years of fighting to vanquish the Spanish Christians, which included the famous guerrilla fighter El Cid. Then Youssef set about taking over the Moorish kingdoms, one by one. With each victory he claimed the wealthy treasuries of the various kingdoms and used them to raise the general standard of living of the people. He abolished high taxes, except on those Jews and Christians who refused to accept Islam, and encouraged science and learning.

Youssef died in 1108, at the age of 101, still in power and in possession of all his faculties. His successors were unable to hold on to the huge sprawling kingdom he had built, however, and Christian forces eventually retook Spain from the Muslims. The influence of Islamic culture would be lasting, however, because while they ruled Spain the Muslims had created a university, public libraries, paved and lighted streets, indoor plumbing, and many other improvements that continued after the Christian takeover.

MANSA
MUSA

(D. 1337)

In the thirteenth century, the Mandinka people of the state of Kangaba in Western Sudan emerged as the most powerful group in Africa. The rise of the Mandinka was due largely to one man, Kankan Musa, who is commonly known as Mansa (Emperor) Musa.

It is not known when Mansa Musa was born, but it is likely that he was the grandson or grandnephew of the legendary Sundiata, who founded the family dynasty. Mansa Musa came to the Mandinka throne in 1312. He oversaw many conquests, including that of Ghana, and created the empire of Mali. Having gained control over the lucrative African gold trade, he set about increasing that trade.

Mansa Musa was a devout Muslim. In 1324, he undertook a pilgrimage to Mecca not only to perform his sacred duty as a Muslim but also to show the power and richness of his kingdom. He set out from his capital of Niani on the Upper Niger River to Walata (present-day Oualâta, Mauritania) and on to Tuat (now in Algeria) before making his way to Cairo, Egypt. He was accompanied by a caravan consisting of sixty thousand men, including twelve thousand slaves. The

emperor himself rode on horseback and was directly preceded by five hundred slaves, each carrying a staff decorated with gold. In addition, Mansa Musa had a baggage caravan of eighty camels, each carrying three hundred pounds of gold. As he passed through Egypt, he paid a visit to Cairo and bestowed fabulous gifts of gold upon the ruler of that city, the sultan Al-Malik an-Nasir of the Mamluks, an Egyptian warrior caste. Mansa Musa did the same when he reached his destination, Mecca.

Rulers of West African states before Mansa Musa had made the pilgrimage to Mecca, but it was his lavish journey that awakened the world to the riches of Mali. Before long, traders from other parts of Africa, the Middle East, and even from as far away as Europe were seeking to do business there.

During Mansa Musa's pilgrimage to Mecca, one of his generals captured the Songhay capital of Gao. Once Gao fell, the rest of the Songhay empire, which consisted of several hundred miles of land in the West African interior, became part of the empire of Mali. Mansa Musa liked to boast that it would take a year for someone to travel from one end of his empire to the other. It was not quite that large; even so, a fourteenth-century traveler named Ibn Battuta reported that it took four months to travel from the northern border of the Mali empire to the capital city of Niani in the south.

When he received word of his new conquest in 1325, Mansa Musa was on his way back to Niani from Mecca. He decided to delay his return to his home in order to visit his newly acquired territory of Gao. There, he planned to preside over the official surrender of the Songhay king and also to take the king's two sons as hostages.

Traveling with Mansa Musa's caravan was Abu Ishaq as-Sahili, a poet and architect from the city of Granada in Spain. Mansa Musa wanted the architect to build mosques for him in his empire. During his pilgrimage, he had been impressed by the architecture of the Arab world, where fired bricks were used instead of the sun-dried bricks common to building in West Africa. In the Arab world, the stronger fired bricks were combined with timber beams, making it possible to construct buildings of more than one story. At both Gao and Timbuktu, another important city in the former Songhay empire, Abu Ishaq as-Sahili designed new mosques, and Mansa Musa is credited with influencing a completely new kind of architecture in his empire.

The great mosque of Sankore was particularly striking. Over the years, it also became a center for the teaching of Islamic philosophy and law, paving the way for the later University of Sankore. In fact, under Mansa Musa, Timbuktu became one of the major cultural centers not only of Africa but of the entire world, with enormous libraries and Islamic universities, a meeting place for the best poets, scholars, and artists of Africa and the Middle East. Even after the power of Mali declined, Timbuktu remained the major Islamic center of sub-Saharan Africa.

The Mali empire was so important that a map of Africa prepared in 1375 by a Spanish mapmaker depicted the emperor of Mali (probably Mansa Musa, even though he had been dead for forty-odd years) seated majestically upon a throne while traders approached his markets.

After the death of Mansa Musa, the power of Mali began to decline. The territory controlled by Mali comprised three distinct regions: the Senegal region with people speaking Niger-Kongo languages, the central Mande states occupied by the Soninke and Mandinka peoples, and the region of Gao occupied by people who spoke Songhay. Subject states began to break away from Mali. In 1430, the Tuareg Berbers in the north seized much of Mali's territory, including the city of Timbuktu. A decade later, the Mossi kingdom to the south seized much of Mali's southern territories. Finally, the kingdom of Gao, which had been subjugated under Mansa Musa, gave rise to a Songhay kingdom that finally eclipsed the magnificent power of Mali.

ASKIA

THE GREAT

(D. 1538)

Songhay was the most notable of the kingdoms that arose in West Africa during the later Middle Ages. At the height of its power, it stretched from the Atlantic Ocean across Central Africa to the borders of the Sudan. Its founder was Sonni Ali. As a young man, he had been pressed into service in Mansa Musa's army after his own Songhay people were conquered around 1324. He escaped and returned to his homeland, where he inspired his people to rise up against Mansa Musa and regain their land. After that success he conquered surrounding territories until he controlled the area from Timbuktu to the Atlantic Ocean. But he never turned his attention to strengthening his kingdom internally.

That task was accomplished by Mohammed ben Abu Bekr. He had been Sonni Ali's favorite general, and he believed he would be a better ruler than Abu Kebr, Ali's son and successor. One year after Abu Kebr succeeded to the throne, Mohammed ben Abu Bekr attacked and defeated him. When one of the daughters of Sonni Ali heard that Abu Bekr had seized the throne, she cried out "Askia!" which means

"usurper." Abu Bekr had a sense of humor; he took Askia as his name.

Known as a generous man with a good heart, Askia set about consolidating his vast empire by ending the conflicts between the various political and religious elements in the kingdom. The Muslim holy men often tried to influence government affairs, but whereas Sonni Ali had tried to suppress them, Askia tried to work with them, to make them feel as if they had influence while keeping that influence to a minimum.

To create closer ties among the various territories, Askia took as wives the daughters of many chiefs. He also married off his daughters to the chiefs whose territory he wanted to keep under his control. He did the same thing with dignitaries and judges until most of the prominent families in his empire were tied to him by marriage.

He organized his kingdom politically by dividing it into four parts and placing a viceroy at the head of each. He also created a regular army, which freed up the rest of the men to pursue commerce, further encouraging trade development by having harbors and canals constructed along the Nile River and its tributaries. Askia maintained a merchant fleet to increase trade and a war fleet to protect the merchant fleet. He sent Songhay ships to Portugal and to Mediterranean ports and welcomed ships from there to his Atlantic ports. He also sent overland caravans to Egypt, Algeria, Morocco, and Iraq.

Askia arranged for the brightest young men in his kingdom to be educated at the great Muslim universities of North Africa, Asia, and Europe. He further developed Timbuktu until it became the most important center of Muslim trade and learning in Africa, often called "The Mecca of the Sudan."

Having stabilized his empire, Askia began to enlarge it, conquering neighboring territories until his territory extended east beyond Lake Chad. But as time went on, he began to lose his sight. He managed to keep his blindness a secret for a while, but eventually the truth leaked out. His subjects did not believe he could govern them successfully, and in the midst of the unrest his son forced him to abdicate. Askia stepped down in 1529 after a reign of more than thirty-six years. But the disloyal son soon died, and Askia directed another son to retake power. He returned to the palace and lived there until he died in 1538.

Timbuktu flourished for another half century before Morocco invaded and conquered the Songhays in 1591. Two hundred years later, another Moorish invasion nearly destroyed the kingdom.

PART TWO

✦

HEROES OF THE STRUGGLE AGAINST EUROPEAN INCURSION

NZINGHA

(1582–1663)

Queen Nzingha of Matamba reigned for thirty-six years in seventeenth-century Angola. She built a strong army and fought several wars against the Portuguese. According to a Dutch ally, she enjoyed fighting, dressed like a man, and even in her old age was as nimble as a young person.

Nzingha, who later became better known as Ann Zingha, was born into a royal family in Angola in southwest Africa. Her brother would later become king. Nzingha was trained as a woman warrior, commonly called an Amazon by English speakers.

Nzingha was born at a time when the Portuguese were establishing a foothold in West Africa in order to engage in trade. They built settlements and forts, and when they could not do so with the cooperation of the local people, they took what they wanted by force. When Nzingha was old enough to do battle, she led her army of fierce women warriors against the Portuguese, but her forces were beaten back. Unlike the Amazons, who fought with spears, the Portuguese had firearms.

Although the Angolan warriors were at a disadvantage because

their weapons were no match for those of the Portuguese, they often managed to hold their own through bravery and sheer numbers. Still, as time went on it became clear to the Angolan king that the best course would be to make peace with the Portuguese. In 1622, he sent his forty-year-old sister Nzingha to Loanda to negotiate peace terms with the Portuguese viceroy there.

In anticipation of the arrival of the royal visitor, the Portuguese made what they thought were appropriate preparations for her lodging and food. When she was ushered into the room where the viceroy received visitors, however, Nzingha was insulted. A magnificent chair of state was in place for the arrival of the viceroy, but she was shown to a pillow in the center of a carpet. The pillow was gold-embroidered velvet, the carpet was the finest Oriental weave, and no doubt the Portuguese believed they were honoring her in arranging that particular

European visitors greeted by the king, who is seated on one of his servants.

seating. But Nzingha was not pleased. Refusing to take a seat on the pillow as expected, she bade one of her attendants to kneel down on her hands and knees, whereupon Nzingha sat on the woman's back and waited for the viceroy's arrival.

When he entered the room, the viceroy was taken aback by the sight of the Amazon using her attendant as a stool, but he soon forgot the unusual seating arrangement as the negotiations proceeded. With great dignity and a royal manner, Nzingha negotiated the best terms she could get under the circumstances. She declined a formal alliance with the Portuguese, which would have required the Angolans to pay an annual tribute, or tax. Instead, she persuaded the viceroy to be satisfied with the Portuguese prisoners whom she offered to give up.

When the negotiations were over, the viceroy got up from his chair to escort his guest from the room. Nzingha rose also, but her "stool" remained in place. When the viceroy mentioned that perhaps she should take her attendant with her, Nzingha responded that it would not be appropriate for the ambassadress of a great king to sit on the same seat twice. "I have no further use for the woman," she said.

Probably more as an act of diplomacy than of faith, Nzingha was baptized as a Christian during her stay in Loanda. Her brother the king died not long after she returned to Angola, and she immediately seized the throne. The Portuguese, thinking that Angola was in a weakened condition because of the change in leadership, sent an army against her.

In response, Queen Nzingha made alliances with neighboring chieftains and with the Dutch, who also had forts and trading facilities in the area. With their aid, she managed to hold her own. The fighting went on for a number of years, but eventually the Portuguese claimed victory. They offered to allow Nzingha to remain on the Angolan throne if she would pay an annual tribute, but she would have none of that. Instead, she escaped. Hiding in the bush country, she gathered another army and fought the Portuguese for another eighteen years.

During those years, she turned against Christianity as the religion of her enemies, took the local missionaries prisoner, and ordered the execution of those among her own people who kept the Christian faith. After her favorite sister died and she began to think of her own advancing years, however, she gave in to the entreaties of her missionary prisoners and adopted Christianity again. Once she did so, the Portuguese offered peace and restored her to the throne.

In the years that followed, Queen Nzingha adopted a number of Christian European ways, including the outlawing of religious sacrifices and polygamy, or the taking of multiple spouses. She even sent a message to the pope in Rome, asking for more Catholic missionaries. To set an example, she married one of her courtiers in a church wedding when she was seventy-six years old. She died five years later. When her body was displayed for her subjects, she was dressed in royal robes, a bow and arrow in her hands. But she was buried in a religious habit instead of the royal robes and a crucifix replaced the bow and arrow.

OSEI
TUTU

(D. 1731)

The Ashanti are said to be the descendants of Ethiopians who were driven south by a conquering Egyptian army more than two thousand years ago. Establishing themselves in West Africa, they gradually extended the boundaries of their territory by taking over neighboring lands. They also developed a trade with the Phoenicians, traders from the east coast of the Mediterranean, at present-day Lebanon. By the middle 1300s they were trading with France, and by the later part of the seventeenth century they also counted England as a trading partner. By this time, the Ashanti were the most powerful group in their area.

Osei Tutu was born some years after the trade with England began, although the date is not known. He was of royal blood, the nephew of the reigning king of the Ashanti, Obiria Yebo. As a youth, Osei Tutu was a shield-bearer to Boa, an overlord of the Ashanti kings. He made the mistake of falling in love with Boa's sister and fathering her child. As a result, Osei Tutu was forced to flee Boa's territory.

In 1697, Osei Tutu succeeded his uncle as king. He established his seat of government at Coomassie and soon earned a reputation for fairness and for listening to his people. He dreamed of expanding his nation and enlisted his cousin Bautin, who was also a king, to join him in a campaign of conquest against their neighbors. He also reorganized his army and introduced the practice of marching in formation.

Learning of the alliance of the cousin kings, King Bosinante, who ruled over Denkera to the west, decided to take action before they tried to invade his lands. He sent a royal delegation, consisting of his favorite wives and most powerful warriors, supposedly to pay tribute to Osei Tutu, but in actuality Bosinante wanted to show off. Osei Tutu received the delegation with courtesy and respect. Not to be outdone, he sent a return delegation composed of his own most beautiful wives. Osei Tutu's chief queen led this delegation. She was an extraordinarily beautiful woman. Bosinante fell in love with her immediately, and she returned the feeling.

When the delegation of wives returned to Coomassie, Osei Tutu realized that his chief queen was pregnant. He was insulted and furious. Apparently, he did not see the irony in the fact that he himself had been forced to flee Denkera in his youth because of a similar offense.

Bosinante offered a large quantity of gold as a peace offering, but Osei Tutu would not have it. He prepared for war. Bosinante died during the preparations, but Tutu did not consider the debt of honor paid. He proceeded with his plans to attack Denkera. The Denkera put up a good fight, aided by their neighbors, the Akim, but the Ashanti were victorious. Among the dead Denkera warriors was Ntim, the Denkera king who was said to have been Osei Tutu's son.

The conquest of Denkera brought great riches to Osei Tutu and the Ashanti nation. Tutu collected an immense amount of gold, which the Denkera had amassed from their very profitable trade with European slavers. The Denkera territory included the land on which the Dutch slave fort, Elmina Castle, had been built and for which the Dutch paid an annual tribute. Under Tutu's rule, the slave trade continued, and Tutu used the riches he amassed to improve the lives of his subjects.

Tutu proceeded to conquer all the neighboring tribes, clans, and villages, uniting them into one kingdom. Each group was expected to pay an annual tribute, or tax, to Tutu, the King of the Ashanti. The Akim, who had allied with the Denkera to fight the original Ashanti invasion, refused to pay their tribute of four thousand ounces of gold, whereupon Tutu sent a large army against them in 1731. On his way to join up with his army, Tutu, accompanied by his wives, children, and lesser nobility, was guarded by only a small group of soldiers. Tutu felt safe because his army had already conquered the territory through which he was traveling. But the Akim somehow learned of his plans and attacked the royal party as it was about to cross the Prah River at Coromantee. Tutu was wounded in the first volley of musket fire. He rose to fight back and was ordering his forces to regroup when a second musket ball killed him. The Akim then attacked and killed the entire royal party of three hundred, including sixty wives. In response, the Ashanti took horrible vengeance on the Akim, burning their city to the ground and killing every living thing in it.

Osei Tutu died on a Saturday. That day and the place of his death became the basis for the most sacred oath, or promise, that a member of the Ashanti nation could make. It was called the Coromantee Saturday Oath, but it was rarely spoken of by that name. Rather, it was called "the great oath of the dreadful day."

In death, Tutu became Osei Tutu "the Great," revered as the founder and first king of the Ashanti Nation.

MOSHESH

(1790?–1870)

Moshesh was born about 1790, in what is now South Africa. His people, the Bafokeng, were a small and comparatively weak group. When he grew up, he became a leader of his people. During the time that Chaka, king of the Zulus, was marauding through the countryside, murdering as many non-Zulu Africans as he could find, Moshesh led his people to the safety of the Drakensberg Mountains. There, in an area rich in wildlife and also fertile for agriculture, Moshesh's people made a new home for themselves. Moshesh established his capital village on a broad plateau high in the mountains and fortified it against attack. When other people fleeing Chaka's onslaught sought refuge in the mountains, Moshesh welcomed them. Gradually, he built up a powerful kingdom called Basuto.

The Basuto were exceptionally fine horsemen, and scholars have compared their skill and courage to the Indians of North America. They needed those qualities in the middle 1830s when the Boers came. The Boers were the descendants of Dutch traders and explorers who had settled in southern Africa and founded Cape Colony at the tip of the continent. In 1836, chafing under British rule and especially

Britain's restrictions on slavery and liberal policies toward native Africans, the Boers left Cape Colony. They moved north in what is known as the Great Trek. Reaching the territory controlled by Moshesh, they seized a large tract of land and founded the Orange Free State. The Orange River Boers, as they came to be called, established farms where they raised livestock and cultivated the land.

Although the Boers had guns and cannons which Moshesh lacked, he did have clever horsemen and an impenetrable mountain fortification. He sent horsemen to raid the Boer farms and drive off their cattle, which he then captured to increase his own herds. The Boers tried to fight back by aiming their cannons at Moshesh's mountain fort, but he unleashed an avalanche of rocks and drove them away. The fighting between the Basuto and the Boers ended in 1843 when the British, who now claimed all of South Africa, made a treaty of peace with Moshesh. Soon afterward, the Boers asked the British to make a peace treaty with them as well.

The British sent Sir Henry George Wakelyn Smith to offer a peace treaty to Moshesh. Sir Harry had served in the Cape area since 1828, most recently as governor of the Province of Queen Adelaide on the eastern frontier of Cape Colony. He apparently considered Africans simpleminded and went through an elaborate pantomime to demonstrate what would happen if Moshesh did not put his mark on the treaty. Smith alternately pretended to snore and to cry, by which he meant to show the peaceful sleep of peace if the treaty were signed and the anguish of war if Moshesh did not. Moshesh was amused by the performance, but he signed the treaty because he understood the grave dangers that confronted him and his people. He had no doubt that the Boers and the British would put aside their enmity and unite against him if it suited their purposes. After all, they were white, and the Basuto were black.

Because of this correct perception, Moshesh decided to deprive the Europeans of one major reason to unite against him: religion. He and his people were animists and thus considered godless pagans by the Europeans. He decided to introduce Christianity into his kingdom and invited missionaries from Europe to teach their religion to his people. His missionary guests were impressed by Moshesh's apparent piety (secretly he held on to his own faith) and sent glowing reports back to Europe.

Meanwhile, Moshesh almost immediately broke the treaty he had signed. Hardly had Sir Harry Smith left Basuto territory when Moshesh ordered an attack on the Boers, seizing ten thousand cattle and twenty-five hundred horses in a series of successful raids. As he had expected, the British and the Boers united against him. The British sent an expedition to rout one of his chiefs at Viervoct. After a terrible battle, the British were thrown back. The governor of Cape Colony, General Sir George Cathcart, then led an army of three thousand Europeans and a large group of Africans to Basutoland. Along the way, the force gathered even more recruits from among the tribes hostile to Moshesh. Reaching the borders of Basutoland, General Cathcart sent a message to Moshesh, demanding that he surrender ten thousand head of cattle. Moshesh sent three thousand head, with a letter (written by a scribe, because Moshesh never learned to read or write) stating that he needed time to gather the rest.

Cathcart refused to wait. He began to march his troops into Basutoland. Approaching a place near the Caledon River called Thaba Bosigo, Cathcart saw a huge herd of cattle feeding on the mountainside, guarded, it seemed, by a group of old women. He divided his forces and sent one unit to round up the cattle, another along the road that led to the heights and Moshesh's stronghold, and kept the third with him below to await developments.

Too late, the force sent to get the cattle realized they had ridden into a trap. They had managed to round up about four thousand head and were driving them down the mountain through a narrow pass when about eight hundred Basuto cavalry attacked them from out of nowhere. Caught in the stampede, the British forces were easy targets. They quickly abandoned the cattle and fled down the mountain toward the general's unit below. But Cathcart's unit was also beset by Basuto horsemen. Only a violent thunderstorm prevented a massacre of the British. Under cover of thunder, lightning, and torrential rain, the British forces retreated across the Caledon River.

Moshesh was smart enough to know that the British Queen Victoria would not take the defeat lightly. She was liable to send a huge force against him in retaliation for the humiliation of her troops on the mountainside. He sent a letter to General Cathcart in which he asked for peace and promised to try to keep his people under control in the future. Cathcart was both astonished and relieved when he read the letter. It gave him the opportunity to feel like a victor, and he took it. Cathcart quickly ordered his forces to depart. They took with them only fifteen hundred head of cattle, but at least they had their pride.

As soon as the British left, the wiley Moshesh sent messages to all the neighboring chiefs taking credit for the departure and announcing a great African victory over the soldiers of the queen. He then set about attacking those chiefs in and around his territory who had aided General Cathcart in the fight against him.

Soon the Basuto and the Boers were at each other again. Angered by Moshesh's growing reputation for piety in Europe, they destroyed several of the Christian missions in Moshesh's kingdom. In fact, for the next twelve years they skirmished off and on. Each time the Boers invaded Basutoland, they were beaten back. Moshesh in his mountain fortress was never in serious danger, and his forces managed to kill two of the leading Boer commanders.

When Moshesh was in his eighties, he took a clever nonmilitary step against the Boers. He decided that the best way to protect his people after he was gone was to place them under the protection of the Boers' main enemy, the British.

Moshesh died in 1870. He was praised in Basutoland and in

Europe as one of the most remarkable African leaders of all time, particularly as a great diplomat. Along with his clever letter to General Cathcart, another incident exemplifies Moshesh's skill as a diplomat as well as a warrior king. Once, having successfully beaten back an attack by the Matabele, a people of Zulu origin who had been driven out of the Transvaal by the Boers, under the great chieftain Mosellikatze, Moshesh did not allow the losing warriors to return to their territory beaten and hungry. Instead, he called them back and gave them food to take home, thereby ensuring peace with them in the future.

CETEWAYO

(1836?–1884)

Also spelled Ketchwayo and Cetshwayo, the name Cetewayo has come down over the last century and a half in African history to mean bravery and excellent character. Cetewayo was king of the Zulus at a time when the British were taking over, or annexing, the Transvaal. The Transvaal, in the northeast part of present-day South Africa, bordering Swaziland, Zimbabwe, and Botswana, was so named because it was situated across the Vaal River as seen from the Cape of Good Hope. From 1910 to 1944, it was a province of South Africa.

Born probably in 1836, Cetewayo was the son of Umpanda, king of the Zulu nation. He was also the grandnephew of Chaka, the founder of the Zulu nation. The Zulu were descendants of the Nguni peoples of southeast Africa who migrated southward to settle in present-day South Africa in the fourteenth and fifteenth centuries. In the early 1800s, Chaka (also known as Shaka), an Nguni chief, had brutally conquered numerous neighboring tribes in Natal and Transvaal in order to form the Zulu nation. Chaka had ensured his power and that of his successors by training an army of warriors renowned for their strength, courage, and brutality.

Young men recruited as Zulu warriors underwent rigorous physical training so that when they were at war they could march as much as fifty miles and then do battle if need be. They were not permitted to marry and had to keep their sole focus on warfare and preparation for war. They were not to show fear or to retreat from danger and were taught to kill their own comrades who did so. The Zulu were feared and hated for good reason all over South Africa.

As a youngster, Cetewayo underwent training as a Zulu warrior. Six-foot-four in height and powerfully built, he dreamed of becoming king of the Zulus. As he grew older, however, he realized that his father, Umpanda, favored his younger brother and planned to choose him as his successor. In 1856, when Cetewayo was only 20 years old, he defeated and killed his younger brother in a battle. Umpanda lived for another sixteen years, but after he died in 1872, Cetewayo became king.

Cetewayo came to power at a time of unrest and change in South Africa. Years earlier, the Boers (Dutch settlers in South Africa) had migrated into Zulu territory in order to be free of British restrictions in the south. At first the Zulu chief Dingaan, Cetewayo's uncle, had welcomed them as fellow enemies of the British. But the Boers had tried to take too much territory, and Dingaan ordered that they be massacred.

The British, who by this time were firmly in control in the south, hoped to enlist the help of Cetewayo against the Boers. They pretended to support his regime, but Cetewayo realized the British intentions and refused to be taken in. He considered both the Boers and the British to be enemies of the Zulu. To protect his people, he banished Christian missionaries from Zululand, accusing them of plotting against him and serving as British spies. In fact, one missionary did write a letter to the governor of Cape Colony, declaring that peace in South Africa could only come with the destruction of the Zulus. When a missionary told Cetewayo that those who refused to believe in God would burn in the fires of hell, he responded that his soldiers would put out the fire.

Cetewayo also drove away a group of Boers who tried to settle in part of his territory. Once the Boers gave up their republic, nothing stood in the way of complete British domination of South Africa but the Zulus. All that Sir Bartle Frere, the British High Commissioner in South Africa, needed was an excuse to wage war against them.

That excuse finally came in 1878. A Zulu chief's wife ran away from Zululand with another man. The chief sent a force that kidnapped her and brought her back, after which she was killed. Frere announced that he would not allow the Zulu to send armies outside their land. He also sent emissaries to Cetewayo with further demands: Zulu warriors were to be permitted to marry (Frere thought they would be less dangerous if they were not so focused on warfare) and a British representative was to be allowed to live in Cetewayo's capital. The final demand was that Cetewayo disband all his forces. In response to these insulting demands, Cetewayo rose from his throne and told the emissaries that he and every one of his men would die first.

In January 1879, a combined British force of twelve thousand, including about twice as many blacks as whites, invaded Zululand at three different locations. British troops had artillery and machine guns; the Zulus had only knives and spears. But the highly disciplined and fearless Zulus charged the British in wave after wave, breaking through the fortifications and finally engaging the British in hand-to-hand combat. At Isandhlwana, thirty-five hundred Zulu were killed, but they in turn killed almost the entire British force of three thousand. Only forty-two escaped by swimming their horses down a stream. The Zulus captured hundreds of rifles and artillery cartridges. At two other points of entry into Zululand, Cetewayo's armies also pushed back the British attack.

In London, Queen Victoria reacted to the news of the defeat of her forces by ordering fifteen thousand soldiers to Cape Colony. These forces invaded Zululand in August 1879. Cetewayo was ready with his own army of twenty-five thousand warriors, but when the two sides met at Ulundi, the outcome was far different from the battle earlier that year. As courageous and determined as they were, the Zulus could not get past the artillery fire coming from the British fortification of ammunition carts and wagons. After losing some five thousand men, Cetewayo reluctantly gave the order to withdraw. The great Zulu War was over.

Cetewayo became a fugitive, traveling across Zululand with a small number of servants and guards, seeking shelter wherever he could find it. He was soon captured and taken to the Cape Colony as a prisoner along with some servants and four of his wives. There he was housed in apartments at the Cape fort and eventually relocated to a farm at Oude Molen. He was treated well and became something of a celebrity, for there were some in the Cape Colony who felt he had just been doing his duty as a ruler and trying to protect his kingdom from invasion.

In Cetewayo's absence, many chiefs in Zululand tried to seize power over the kingdom. In some ways it was now more of a threat to the British than when Cetewayo had been in power. The region was beset by such unrest that at last Queen Victoria granted Cetewayo's request to travel to England to meet with her. In July 1882, after three years of captivity, he departed for England.

Cetewayo was received in London as a respected head of state and a guest of the British government. Aware that he would be better accepted if he dressed in the European manner, he wore a suit, a silk top hat, and gloves. Crowds turned out to see him, and delegations from many learned societies visited him. He was taken to visit places of interest and showered with gifts. Best of all, Queen Victoria promised to restore him to power.

Anxious to return to his homeland, Cetewayo took leave of his new British friends and went back to Africa in 1883, only to find that despite the queen's promises, all of Zululand was no longer his to govern. Pressed by the British in South Africa, authorities in England had authorized the division of the kingdom into three parts, only one of which was restored to him.

In a first step toward reuniting his kingdom, Cetewayo declared war on a rival chief, Usibepu. But the British backed Usibepu, and Cetewayo's forces were defeated. Discredited in the eyes of his subjects, Cetewayo lost all hope of regaining power. He died in February 1884, possibly of heart trouble, but perhaps of poisoning. It was a sad ending for a great king who had handed England the worst defeat it had ever experienced in Africa.

Portrait of the Zulu king Cetewayo.

KHAMA

(D. 1923?)

Khama was the oldest son and heir of Sekhomi, chief of the Bamangwato, a branch of the Bantu peoples. At the time of Khama's birth, Sekhomi was *kgosi* or paramount chief of a large territory in northern South Africa called Bechuanaland. Kgosi Sekhomi practiced the traditional religion of prayer to many different gods. In fact, he was a very skilled and feared sorcerer.

Young Khama grew tall and strong, becoming a fast runner and a skilled and fearless hunter. The Bamangwato people were pleased that Khama was heir to the throne and would rule Bechuanaland one day.

But while still a young man, Khama began to have strong differences with his father. He rejected his father's religion and adopted Christianity. He criticized his father for welcoming white traders, who brought whiskey and chaos into the territory. Whereas his father had killed one of his own brothers and tried to kill another of his own sons, Khama was against violence and bloodshed. The differences between father and son eventually became so great that Khama gave up his right to succeed his father as chief of the Bamangwato and left his father's capital, Shoshong.

But the people of Shoshong had come to love the gentle prince and they clamored for his return. Not wanting unrest in his capital, Sekhomi asked his son to come back. Khama did so reluctantly and soon regretted his decision, because father and son continued to disagree. When Sekhomi tried to arrange for Khama to marry the daughter of a powerful chief, he refused. He was already married to a Christian girl of the Bamangwato, and as a Christian did not believe in having more than one wife.

Not wanting to anger his father into breaking off their relationship again, he showed his obedience by offering to perform the most difficult task his father could assign. But his father would not accept Khama's offer as a substitute for an arranged marriage. Furious, Sekhomi went to his son Macheng and offered to make him his heir to the throne in exchange for killing his brother. Since Macheng was the son whom Sekhomi had once tried to kill, he did not trust his father and refused.

Relations between Khama and his father were still at an impasse when Lobenguela, the most powerful of the neighboring kings, prepared to attack Sekhomi's land with a force of several thousand warriors. Sekhomi decided to rely on magic and gathered together all the most powerful sorcerers to cast their spells against Lobenguela. Khama scoffed at the gathering as nonsense and announced to his father, "It is time to fight."

He gathered a small force of young men and went out to meet Lobenguela's forces, fighting so bravely and cleverly that he forced the enemy into retreat. Shortly afterward, Khama's brother Khamana also converted to Christianity. Now Sekhomi had two sons who refused to take part in the traditional rites that he held dear. Furious at Khama, he commanded his warriors to set fire to Khama's hut when Khama was asleep inside. When they refused, he tried to fire his rifle into the hut, but the warriors knocked it away so that the shots went wild.

Sekhomi finally had to admit that he had lost his authority.

He ran away, because according to tribal law Khama now had the right to kill him. But Khama chose not to exercise that right. Instead, he honored the Christian teaching to forgive his enemies and sent a messenger to his father, inviting him back to the capital.

Quiet for a time, Sekhomi's hatred of Christianity and the new ways his sons were adopting led him to plan a revolt. He assembled several hundred tribesmen who were still loyal to him and made plans to attack Khama. But Khama refused to do battle with his father and left of his own accord, accompanied by his brother Khamana and all the Christians of the tribe. They settled in a fortified place in the mountains, where Sekhomi tried to attack them and was beaten off.

Back in Shoshong, the people clamored for Khama's return, and eventually Sekhomi invited him back, only to resume plotting against him. He again entreated his son Macheng to kill Khama, and when this time Macheng agreed, Sekhomi abdicated in favor of Macheng. Khama escaped. Not long afterward, Sekhomi had to flee as well, for Macheng tried to poison him.

Under Macheng, who was not a good leader, Bechuanaland fell into chaos as various chiefs began to jockey with one another for power. Secheng, chief of the Bakwena, attacked and captured Macheng and ordered that he be shot. But Khama, who kept current on what was happening in the capital, interceded on his brother's behalf. Instead of being killed, Macheng was banished from the tribe. He died shortly afterward.

By popular demand, Khama returned to become paramount chief, taking the name Kgosi Khama III. But then his brother Khamana, urged on by their father, began to plot against him. So Khama left again, along with more than half the tribe. He relocated to Serowe, some seventy miles away, where he built his own town. Pretty soon, word came that Khamana wanted him back, but Khama had had enough. He refused, and only after others back in Shoshong begged him to do so did he return to the capital. This time he arrested both Khamana and his father.

Khama then set about driving out the old traditions and superstitions, putting an end to rainmaking ceremonies and substituting Christian services for pagan rites. He banished the whiskey traders, built schools, established a mounted police force, and introduced scientific improvements in agriculture. He ordered that the old and the sick be cared for and took the weaker tribes under his protection. To show that he meant business, he married one of his own daughters to the chief of the lowliest tribe, the Makalala.

By 1895, however, pressure from the whiskey traders and the railroad builders was so great that he traveled to London to plead with Queen Victoria for her help in keeping what he considered evil forces out of his territory. He was received in London with great respect and all the honors due to a king, and Queen Victoria confirmed his right to control what went on in Bechuanaland.

Kgosi Khama III presided over a peaceful kingdom, his power unthreatened, for many more years, and in the fiftieth year of his reign was honored with a great celebration. Three years after that, in 1925, a monument was built in his honor at Serowe. On its base were the words "Righteousness exalteth a nation." Seven years later, while riding on horseback through a thunderstorm, he caught a cold, which developed into pneumonia. He was said to be 104 years old when he died.

BOWELLE

(1841–1906)

Behanzin, whose surname meant "The King Shark," was born into the royal family of the Dahomey in West Africa in the middle nineteenth century. His family line stretched back to 1610 when a chief named Tacodounon took the country's throne. Behanzin was tall and well built and carried himself in a dignified manner. His most remarkable accessory was a long pipe, which he pulled on thoughtfully as he pondered his rulings or a new line of poetry. An accomplished poet, he composed war chants as well as romantic verse. Like Dahomean *dadas* (kings) before him, Behanzin had absolute power over a kingdom that was rich from trade and defended by an army of twenty-five thousand warriors, five thousand of whom were women.

Behanzin recognized that the major threat to his power and to his country was France. In 1626, France had sought to establish a sphere of influence in Dahomey. Louis XIII, the king of France, had sent Admiral D'Elbee to visit the king to negotiate a trade agreement. As a result, France was allowed to establish a trading post on the coast of Dahomey. The relationship between Dahomey and France had

remained close and mutually beneficial for more than two centuries. In 1868, Behanzin's father, Gli-Gli, made a treaty that gave France the Dahomean port of Cotonou.

Although Dahomey grew wealthy from its trade with France, Behanzin was concerned that France was getting the better deal. In 1890, he negotiated a new treaty that called for France to pay him an annual rent of twenty thousand francs' worth of gold for the use of Cotonou port. He was also worried that France had designs on the rest of his country, not just its coast, and decreed that no white people be allowed in the interior. In the rare cases where exceptions were made, he forbade surveying equipment or cameras. Explorers, for example, were treated with great respect but were accompanied by guides who showed them only what the king wanted them to see. To increase the effectiveness of his defense forces, he sought the help of Germany, which was also interested in gaining influence in Africa. Germany supplied him with rifles, and five Germans held high rank in his army.

In 1890, the French defied Behanzin and tried to send an expedition into the interior of Dahomey. Behanzin's army was able to turn back the expedition. He then declared that the treaty between France and Dahomey was null and void and that the French must get out of Cotonou. France tried to negotiate with Behanzin, but he refused to accept the gifts their envoys tried to press upon him. Several armed engagements took place in which Behanzin's forces were victorious.

Then France turned to its best fighter in Africa, the half-French, half-Senegalese Colonel A. A. Dodds. Dodds sent Behanzin a letter demanding that he submit to the terms France wanted. Behanzin replied that France was the only European nation that he would not deal with. The war resumed. Strong and courageous as they were, Behanzin's troops proved no match for the French artillery and Colonel Dodds's Senegalese sharpshooters. In addition, King Toffa of Porto-Novo was fighting on the side of the French. Dioxene, Behanzin's largest palace, fell to the enemy.

After two neighboring peoples, the Egbas and the Gesus, joined the French in fighting Dahomey, Behanzin decided it was time to make peace. He sent three representatives to Colonel Dodds, offering the French five million francs' worth of gold and free use of the port of Cotonou. Dodds responded that he was willing to make peace only if Behanzin gave up his capital city of Abomey. Behanzin refused and the war resumed. As enemy forces advanced on Abomey, Behanzin ordered it burned down rather than see it taken by the French. He then fled.

Dodds's forces took over what was left of Abomey, and Dodds named Behanzin's brother, Agli-Agbo, king. Dodds then set sail for France, thinking that the situation in Dahomey was under control. He had barely arrived, however, when word came that Behanzin had rallied what was left of his loyal forces and was trying to take the throne from his brother. Dodds returned to defeat Behanzin once and for all.

On January 24, 1894, Behanzin walked into Dodds's camp and surrendered. Taken to France, he was later exiled to the island of Martinique. He tried for many years to get permission to return to his native land, but the closest he got was Algeria, where he died in 1906 at the age of sixty-five. In 1928, his son, Prince Ouanilo Behanzin, finally returned his father's body to Dahomey for burial.

Although he failed in the end, Behanzin heroically kept his kingdom independent of any European power at a time when neighboring rulers had given in. He is remembered as one of the great kings of Africa.

RABAH

(D. 1900)

Rabah was born in the Sudan of a poor, illiterate people. Like his mother, he was a slave. Around 1860, he was captured at Bahr el Ghazal on the Upper Nile and sold as a slave in Egypt. The man who bought him was named Zobeir, who soon after was hired by a French woman, Mademoiselle Tinne, to serve as her guide on an expedition up the Nile. Zobeir took his slave Rabah with him, for Rabah was tall and strong and very intelligent.

To defend her party on the expedition, Mademoiselle Tinne had purchased guns and ammunition. At the end of the trip, she gave it all to Zobeir, who decided to use the gift to establish himself as a slave trader. He took on some fellow adventurers as partners and got together a slave-hunting expedition to Rabah's homeland in the Sudan. Rabah accompanied the expedition.

Zobeir's slave-trading business was so successful that he established his own kingdom in the Sudan, which displeased the Egyptians. Egypt, which had been under the indirect control of Great Britain for years, was in the process of conquering the Sudan at the time (1870s). Egyptian forces made war on Zobeir, but Rabah, who by this time had risen to the position of second-in-command under his

master, managed to repulse all attacks. The Egyptians offered a peace treaty under which Zobeir would become a viceroy. Zobeir signed the treaty and accepted an invitation to travel to Cairo, Egypt, for a celebration in his honor. Immediately on his arrival in Cairo, however, he was imprisoned on orders from British Gen. Charles George Gordon.

Zobeir's son Suleyman and Rabah had stayed behind in Sudan. On learning what happened to Zobeir, they once again attacked the Egyptians. This time they were not successful in battle. The Egyptians sent word that if they surrendered, their lives would be spared. Suleyman took the Egyptians at their word, surrendered, and was executed. Rabah was suspicious of the offer and declined it. In 1879, when the Egyptians came after him, he gathered seven hundred black slave soldiers and escaped on fast horses into the desert.

As fugitives, Rabah and his followers had no way to support themselves. They soon resorted to attacking and plundering the trade caravans that crossed the Sahara Desert on their way to the Mediterranean port of Tripoli. Over the years Rabah grew wealthy from plunder and established his own kingdom, in what is now the nation of Chad. He then began adding to his territory by making war on neighboring kingdoms, including the Snussi, the Wadai, and the Sakara. Finally, he set his sights on Bornu, located on the western shores of Lake Chad.

This wealthy kingdom had grown accustomed to peace and was not prepared for Rabah's attack. Its army was made up mostly of slaves whose commanders were former captives. Rabah sent only two thousand men to make war against fifteen thousand of the Bornuese soldiers and was victorious in 1883. This greatly alarmed England, France, Belgium, and Germany, as they had territory bordering that of Rabah. The French were the first to send an expedition against him, in 1899. Rabah repulsed it, killed its leader, and captured all the arms and ammunition of the French forces. He then headed south to defeat a similar German expedition.

After the annexation of Bornu, Rabah's territory was larger than France and Germany combined. He now set about consolidating his power over it. He reorganized Bornu into a military dictatorship, rebuilt its towns, and encouraged the resumption of trade. He made the former Bornuese capital of Dikoa his capital. The French continued to try to attack him, but these efforts did not have the support of many in France, where a leading newspaper had even complained that Rabah had a right to defend his own kingdom. In 1899, Rabah was again victorious over a French incursion.

Feeling threatened on his southern border by the Germans, who controlled Tanganyika, Rabah soon invaded German territory, leaving most of his cavalry behind in Bornu to guard his territory there. The French decided he was in a weak position and, after securing German permission to attack Rabah on German territory, attacked him at Kussuri. Rabah held out on a fortified hillside until he ran out of ammunition, then left the hill to go on the attack. His forces were slaughtered, and Rabah himself, nursing wounds in the bushes, was slain by a deserter from his own army.

The French paid tribute to him as the most remarkable adversary they had encountered in Africa.

MENELIK II

(1844–1913)

Given that Ethiopia is an ancient kingdom, it is no surprise that its royal family traces its line back thousands of years. The family of Menelik II went all the way back to 930 BC. Only once in the long history of the Menelik line had the family been deprived of power in Ethiopia. In AD 950 the Falashas, or Ethiopian Jews, had wrested control of the throne. The Menelik line had reasserted itself and resumed its rule. But when Menelik II was born in 1844, the dominance of the family had again been threatened.

Ethiopian kings took different names when they assumed the throne. Menelik II was born Sahaba Mariem. He was eleven years old in 1855, when Kassai, a man of humble birth, killed his father and took over the throne. Crowned as King Theodore (or Tewodros II), Kassai then went after the heirs of the king he had just killed. People who were still loyal to the former royal family spirited young Sahaba away to safety. At Shoa, in central Ethiopia, they showed their determination to restore the old monarchy by crowning the adolescent with the ancient title of Elect of God, King of Kings of Ethiopia, Sultan of the Nile, Ever Victorious Lion of Judah. But his only "empire" was Shoa and its environs.

As Sahaba grew older, he tried on several occasions to lead an armed force against King Theodore, but he was always beaten back. It was the British who in 1868 finally unseated the king. Theodore had ordered some British missionaries killed, and in retaliation the British invaded. Theodore committed suicide rather than fall into British hands. His son John (or Emperor Johannes IV), succeeded to the throne. Sahaba also tried to go against him but failed. Meanwhile, he faced attack from British-led Egyptians eager for his territory. He managed to beat them back twice, in 1875 and 1876. In 1882 he made a peace treaty with John. Under the agreement, he would succeed to the throne after John and John's son Ras Area would be Sahaba's successor. To help ensure the success of the agreement, Sahaba married his daugher Zeodita to Ras Area. Not long afterward, both John and his son died—John in a battle and Ras of an illness. In 1889, Sahaba at last became emperor of all Ethiopia. He took the royal name of King Menelik II as a signal that he intended to restore the power and prestige of ancient Ethiopia.

About six feet tall and very heavy, Menelik II carried himself with great dignity and was courteous to everyone, even the lowliest person in his kingdom. He had great plans to make his country a model of Christianity and an example of an African nation that could withstand European encroachment.

For years, however, he was forced to concentrate on merely keeping his throne. John's illegitimate son, Ras Mangascha, wanted to be king and made a treaty with the British to get arms and money to pursue his cause. Menelik II fought off Ras Mangascha for eight years.

The dervishes were his next foe. They were a Muslim group that expressed their spirituality in whirling dances. The dervishes had managed to drive England out of the Sudan and were anxious also to control the headwaters of the Blue Nile, which was in Ethiopian territory. But in three separate campaigns in 1885, 1888, and 1889, Menelik II managed to be victorious over the dervishes.

While he was fighting off the dervishes, Menelik II had Italy to contend with. Trying to gain a foothold in Africa like other European nations, Italy had first invaded Ethiopia in 1869, when John was king. John was also fighting the dervishes at the time and was unable to prevent Italy from seizing some of his territory. Twenty years later, Menelik II found himself in the same position of having to fight off multiple invaders, for in addition to the dervishes, Mangascha and other Ethiopian chiefs were anxious to seize his throne. He decided to enlist the help of the Italians in fighting his other foes. He promised Italy a strip of territory called Asmara in return for one million dollars. Under the Treaty of Uccialli, Italy provided aid, which enabled Menelik II to defeat Mangascha.

Menelik II's empire now extended from the Nile to Lake Victoria and was at peace at last. He set about changing the old order, in which the landowning nobility held most of the power and could abuse at will the people who lived on their lands. He established a strong, centralized government with its seat at Addis Ababa. He treated all his subjects fairly. He set up a postal system and courts of justice, and he regulated duties and taxes. He attempted to end slavery and, when he was unsuccessful, established controls against the abuses of slavery. He built a railroad. He lived simply, and during times of famine would refuse to eat meat because the poor of his kingdom could not afford it. But he expected to be treated like the royal personage he was, and when a representative from a European nation came to call, he rebuked him if he were not properly dressed or respectful.

Neither the Italians nor the British were happy about having an independent Ethiopia in their midst. In fact, in the 1890s Britain and Italy agreed that Ethiopia should be placed under Italian influence. Italy accomplished that shift of power by secretly making two versions of a treaty with Menelik II. One version made Ethiopia a protectorate of Italy. When Menelik II started to make treaties with other European nations, such as France, Austria, and France, Italian King

Humbert protested that the treaty Menelik had signed prevented him from doing so. Menelik II denounced the treaty and refused to abide by its provisions. Italy then invaded Ethiopia and offered support to Mangascha and other chiefs who sought to defeat Menelik.

Menelik understood that not merely his own power but also the independence of Ethiopia were at stake. He sent messengers throughout the land, asking all Ethiopians, whether they were friendly to him or not, to put aside their differences and help him defeat the foreign invaders. A huge force met him at Boromeda, and in a rousing speech he underscored the importance of the battle to come:

> We cannot permit our integrity as a Christian and civilized nation to be questioned, nor the right to govern our empire in absolute independence. . . . The Emperor of Ethiopia is a descendant of a dynasty that is three thousand years old—a dynasty that during all of that time has never submitted to an outsider. Ethiopia has never been conquered and she never shall be. We will call no one to our defense. We are capable of protecting ourselves. Ethiopia will stretch forth her hands only to God.

Italy and Ethiopia fought from 1895 to 1896. The decisive battle took place at Adua where Ethiopia finally crushed the Italian forces. Although he had lost between six thousand and eight thousand men, Menelik had done what no other African leader had—decisively beat back an outside invader. Other European nations then hastened to make formal treaties with Menelik.

Over the next two decades, Menelik's health gradually failed, and as he weakened so did his control. Great intrigue marked the end of his life and reign in 1911. His son and logical successor, Ras Michael, had converted to Islam and could not be emperor of a Christian nation. So Ras Michael's son, Menelik's grandson Lidj Yassu, succeeded to the throne. His grandnephew, Haile Selassie, became emperor in 1928.

BAMBAATA

(1865–1906)

Bambaata was born into the Zondi tribe, part of the Zulu nation of South Africa. As a boy, he displayed the characteristics of the Zulu in that he was tall and strong and liked to fight. He grew up to become the chief of his tribe, which at a total of fifty-five hundred people was small and powerless compared to other tribes in the region.

At that time, the British had pushed the Boers out of Cape Colony and into Zululand. Angry over the encroachment of Boer farmers into his people's territory, Bambaata led raids on Boer farms, seizing their cattle. Meanwhile, the Boers were still fighting the British for control of South Africa. After the three-year Boer War (1899 to 1902), the British were victorious and took control over all of South Africa.

The British authorities in South Africa then tried to pay some of their war debts by taxing the native Africans within their borders. In addition to a hut tax of fifteen dollars and a tax on dogs, they levied a tax on every male adult. Bambaata's people lived in a total of 1,142 huts and had many dogs. They were already poor, and paying such taxes would make them worse off. He declared that his people would not pay the taxes.

He was summoned to the headquarters of the local British governor,

but he refused to go. The government then ordered that he be deposed as chief of the Zondi and declared that a member of the tribe named Magwababa was the new chief. Brtitish police arrived to seize Bambaata but retreated when he threatened to kill them. When the British sent one hundred seventy white soldiers supported by a troop of native Africans, Bambaata fled into Zululand to seek the aid of the paramount chief of the Zulu, Dinizulu.

Dinizulu sympathized with Bambaata, but he'd had his own troubles with the British. In 1889 he was exiled to St. Helena Island in punishment for his own revolt. Allowed to return to Zululand on the promise of good behavior, he could not afford to anger the authorities again. But he said he would secretly help Bambaata. He ordered his best general, Cakijana, to accompany Bambaata, and the two traveled through Zululand and Natal, gathering recruits for a revolutionary force.

They encountered a great deal of reluctance among older Zulus who had faced or heard about European firearms and knew how destructive they could be. One exception was Sigananda, a Zulu chief who was ninety-six years old. Nearly seventy years earlier, he had been one of the leaders of a historic massacre of whites in Natal led by Chief Dingaan. He had seen what European firearms could do, but his hatred of whites was so strong that he didn't care.

Eventually, Bambaata gathered an army of some twelve thousand men. Their weaponry included only twenty rifles; the rest were spears, knives, and clubs. In July 1905, Bambaata returned to his home and ousted Magwababa, the man the British had installed as chief in his place. A government force of several hundred went after him, but in a series of clever ambushes his men killed enough of them to set the others to retreat.

A few days later, another British force attacked Bambaata's village, bombarding the huts with artillery fire. Once again, Bambaata ordered a series of clever ambushes and beat them back.

Now the British authorities realized they had a formidable foe in Bambaata. They sent an army of five thousand men, including whites and blacks, under the command of General Sir Donald McKenzie. The blacks in this force wore black-and-white stripes to distinguish them from the other native Africans. Alerted to their coming, Bambaata arranged for some of his men to wear black-and-white stripes and to serve as his spies. Learning of the maneuvers General McKenzie planned, he again arranged for effective ambushes.

These successive victories on the part of Bambaata caused many other local chiefs to believe that the British could, in fact, be beaten. About twenty of them joined him and offered their armies. Together, these forces fought the British a number of times, charging the British artillery and being mowed down by cannon fire. Unable to get to the enemy to engage in the hand-to-hand combat at which they excelled, they were doomed.

In April 1906, Bambaata was alone near Mome Gorge, making his way along a river, when a native soldier fighting for the British jumped from behind a tree and plunged a spear into his back. He then tried to pull the spear out to stab Bambaata again. But the power of the first thrust had been so great that the spear had bent. Another native soldier came to help him, but Bambaata seized the second man's spear and used it to attack them both. Then a third man appeared and shot Bambaata in the head with his rifle.

Without Bambaata's leadership the rebellion soon collapsed. Nevertheless, it had lasted nine months and cost the British millions of pounds, not to mention the lives of those killed in action. Bambaata's forces had suffered greater casualties, and nearly five thousand had been taken prisoner. Among them were several of the chiefs who had joined Bambaata. Sigananda, the oldest, died a few days after he was captured. Most of the others were sent into exile on St. Helena Island. The exiles included Dinizulu, paramount chief of the Zulu, who was suspected of having aided Bambaata.

Bambaata had been more successful than anyone could have dreamed, and many among his own tribe and other Zulus refused to believe he was dead. Even his wife would not go into mourning. But eventually they came to the sad conclusion that even the courage and cunning of Bambaata had not been enough to overcome the superior weaponry of the British.

PART THREE

◆

HEROES OF THE TWENTIETH CENTURY

H A I L E
SELASSIE

(1891–1988)

Born Tafari Makonnen into the ruling family of Ethiopia, Haile Selassie (who took this name when he became king) claimed direct descent from the kings who had reigned over the land thousands of years before. He was the grandnephew of Menelik II. His father Ras Makonnen, a nephew of Menelik II, had distinguished himself in Ethiopia's war against Italy in 1896, in which Ethiopia won.

Young Selassie showed himself capable of leadership at an early age and was only fourteen when Menelik named him governor of the province of Garamoulata. After the death of his father, however, Menelik called him to live at the royal court in Addis Ababa. There he studied under Ethiopian and European tutors until Menelik appointed him to another governorship. He was still in his teens when he received his third appointment, as governor of Ethiopia's most important province, Harrar. Small in stature—he was only about five feet tall—with finely chiseled features, he was big in character, dignity, and heart.

By this time Menelik was aging and in poor health, and there was much political intrigue at the court as various relatives and ministers jockeyed for power. Selassie was regarded by some as a threat and was removed from the governorship of Harrar and sent to a distant province. Later he was restored to Menelik's favor.

On Menelik's death in 1911, his grandson Lidj Yassu became emperor. Menelik's son and Lidj Yassu's father, Ras (Prince) Michael, was passed over because he had adopted the Muslim faith and could not rule a country that was officially Christian. Lidj Yassu was not officially a Muslim, and when he assumed the throne he took the pledge that Ethiopian rulers had taken for sixteen hundred years, which was to uphold Christianity. Nevertheless, he showed Muslim leanings. For example, he wore a fez, the headwear that had originated in Turkey and was traditional for Muslim men.

During World War I, Lidj Yassu saw an opportunity to rid Africa of British dominance and allied Ethiopia with Germany against the British. He also tried to unite the Christian and Muslim countries of Africa against England and her allies. In so doing, however, he risked incurring the enmity of England and its ally France. The *abuna*, or head of the Ethiopian church, felt he had made a rash decision, enlisted the support of other Ethiopian leaders, and deposed him. In his place they elevated Zaiditu, a daughter of Menelik II, to the throne and named Haile Salassie heir to the throne and regent.

Ras Michael, Lidj Yassu's father, then gathered a large army and marched against the Christian forces. In a great battle at Sagalle in October 1916, in which Haile Selassie was one of the generals, Yassu was defeated. Five years later he made another attempt to seize the Ethiopian throne, but Haile Selassie defeated him again and took him prisoner.

Between 1917 and 1928 Selassie traveled to such cities as Rome, Paris, and London, the first Ethiopian ruler ever to go abroad. In 1923, as Prince Regent Tafari, Selassie took Ethiopia into the League of

Nations, a body established after World War I to try to solve international problems with a form of world government. By agreement, none of the nations in the league could attack any of the others, which seemed at the time to be a wise move.

Selassie then launched a program of modernization, introducing the telephone, the airplane, the telegraph, and reforms in the old system of government. His attempts to force his ancient culture into the modern world were opposed by Empress Zaiditu and her party as well as by the powerful Christian clergy. They argued that modernization meant inviting further European influence, which had deprived so many African nations of their independence. Selassie responded that Ethiopia was surrounded by European influence and could best control it by adopting some of it.

Selassie had powerful people on his side, and in 1928 he was crowned negus, or king. Empress Zaiditu continued to hold nominal power. Two years later, however, her husband Ras Guksa revolted, and in putting down the revolt Haile Selassie's forces killed him. Her husband's death proved to be such a shock to the empress that she also died. Haile Selassie succeeded to the throne and for the first time took the name Haile Selassie, meaning "Might of the Trinity."

He continued his reforms, introducing a parliament and a modern court system, building roads, hospitals, and schools, and installing streetlights. He also abolished slavery in a deliberate, step-by-step manner. First, he freed all the slaves in his palace, after which he introduced laws calling for the gradual abolition of slavery elsewhere in the empire. In 1935 he issued a proclamation abolishing slavery forever. All the while, he tried to keep peace among the many factions in his land, including powerful rulers of provinces who sought to aggrandize themselves.

That same year, Italy, under the dictator Benito Mussolini, invaded Ethiopia. Selassie and his forces fought valiantly, but they were overwhelmed by the superior weaponry of the Italians. In April 1936, after his capital Addis Ababa was captured, he went to Geneva, Switzerland, headquarters of the League of Nations, to put his case before that world body.

In spite of the grand promises with which the League had been formed, economic concerns outweighed moral ones. The member nations were afraid of losing their trade with Italy. Beginning with France, one by one the nations sided with Mussolini. They would later regret doing so. Unable to persuade the League to take his side, Haile Selassie became an emperor without a country. He went into exile in England, living in the seacoast town of Bath as Mr. Tafari but never giving up hope that he would one day be able to return to his throne.

Three years later, in September 1939, the chancellor of Germany Adolf Hitler invaded Poland, setting off World War II. Mussolini sided with Hitler, leading Prime Minister Winston Churchill of England to declare that Haile Selassie was the legal ruler of Ethiopia and pledging British assistance to him to retake his country.

In the summer of 1940, Selassie traveled to Egypt and from there to the Sudan, where he met with British generals and made plans to drive the Italians out of Ethiopia. He fought alongside the British and on May 6, 1941, entered Addis Ababa in triumph.

After the end of World War II, Ethiopia became a founding member of the United Nations (UN). In 1953, after his aid from Britain wound down, Selassie sought aid from other nations in the UN, including the United States, Italy, China, West Germany, Taiwan, Yugoslavia, Sweden, and the Soviet Union.

In 1957, Selassie introduced a limited form of democracy in Ethiopia, to the great consternation of many powerful religious and government leaders. While Selassie was abroad on one of his frequent diplomatic missions, a coup d'état occurred in Addis Ababa in December 1960. The takeover, led by the Imperial Bodyguard, police chief, and intellectual radicals, lacked the necessary public support, and fell upon the return of the emperor.

Selassie was the most respected black ruler in the world. In 1963, he presided over a conference of the heads of state of thirty-two African nations at which the Organization of African Unity was formed. Its primary aim was to "decolonize" the remaining bastions of white rule in Southern Rhodesia, South Africa, Mozambique, and Angola. The following year he visited Jamaica, whose population was primarily the descendants of slaves brought from Africa. In fact, a cult of Jamaicans that called themselves Rastafarians (after the title Selassie held as prince, Ras Tafari), believed him to be the incarnation of God.

While he enjoyed great respect and influence elsewhere in the world, Selassie was losing them at home. In the early 1970s, a severe drought led to a prolonged famine during which hundreds of thousands of people died. The drought caused a variety of economic problems, and an increasingly discontented population accused Selassie and members of the government and the aristocracy of trying to cover them up. Especially in the cities, people began to organize into labor unions and political groups to fight for their rights and better living conditions. In January 1974 Selassie's own army mutinied, taking control in several provinces. In early June, a group of about one hundred twenty military officers formed a group known as the Derg (committee) and began arresting members of the aristocracy and parliament members whom they accused of corruption and cover-up. By the end of the summer they had nationalized, or taken over, Selassie's estate and palace. On September 12, they formally deposed and arrested him. In August 1975, Selassie died under questionable circumstances while under house arrest, and was secretly buried.

Mengistu Haile Mariam, who believed in the economic theories of communism, emerged from the chaos of Selassie's overthrow in 1974 and ran the country until 1991. During those years, Selassie's legend grew around the world. Rastafarians, in particular the Jamaican singer Bob Marley, kept his memory alive through music. A growing number demanded that Selassie's remains be given a dignified burial.

Finally, in 1992, twenty-five years after Selassie's death, the leader of Ethiopia, Prime Minister Meles Zenawi, allowed the reburial of Selassie's remains in Holy Trinity Cathedral in Addis Ababa. Although singer Bob Marley's widow attended the ceremony, comparatively few Rastafarians were there, for they believe him to be God and that he still lives.

The official opinion of the Ethiopian government was that Selassie had been a tyrant and an oppressor, which he may indeed have been in order to retain power and remake his nation as he felt was necessary. But in his time there was no greater champion of an independent Africa and no more powerful African leader than the man known the world over as the "little emperor."

Emperor Haile Selassie playing with his dogs at home in Debre Zeit, Ethiopia.

JOMO
KENYATTA

(1891–1978)

North Africa was a major theater in World War II during the years 1942 and 1943, when the Axis powers Germany and Italy invaded Egypt, Ethiopia, and Tunisia and were engaged by British and American forces. Although southern Africa was not directly affected by the fighting, the war gave rise to new political movements, which grew and flourished after the war ended in 1945. Africans under European domination then began to agitate for freedom and self-determination. They hated racial discrimination and white settlement without assimilation and they were tired of feeling unwanted in their own countries, except as servants for white people. These individual independence movements were so numerous that it seemed as if a wide swath of the continent had been swept up in a single wave of freedom. But each European colony in Africa had its distinctive qualities, as did the leaders of the various decolonization movements, approaching the freedom campaign and realizing their dreams for their new nations in different ways.

Jomo Kenyatta, the first president of independent Kenya, was born Kamau wa Ngengi. He did not become Jomo Kenyatta until 1938, when he published a book under that name. He was born into the Kikuyu tribe, the most influential group in Kenya, whose territory is centered in the Great Rift Valley that runs through the center of the country from Lake Rudolf in the north to Lake Victoria in the south.

When Kenyatta was born, Kenya was controlled by Great Britain. He attended elementary school and learned carpentry at a mission operated by the Church of Scotland. On completing his education in 1912, he became an apprentice carpenter. But there were few jobs available to him, and in 1914 he set out for Nairobi, the capital city, to seek employment.

While he was in Nairobi, World War I broke out. In 1917, the British government in Kenya ordered all able-bodied Kikuyu men to join the armed services, but Kenyatta evaded the draft by moving to an area in the southern part of the country. After the war ended, he returned to Nairobi and got a job as a clerk in a store. He married Grace Wahu, also a Kikuyu, in a traditional ceremony. Later, the British magistrate ordered the couple to get married again in a civil ceremony.

Like many other nonwhite Kenyans, Kenyatta chafed under British control. In 1924, he joined the Kikuyu Central Association (KCA), a political party. Two years later, he took the position of secretary of the KCA. He eventually became editor of a Kikuyu weekly newspaper, *Mwigwithania* (The Reconciler.) He also worked closely with activists in Nairobi's East Indian community. In 1929, he and a local Indian leader named Isher Dass sailed to Great Britain to present petitions to the British government on behalf of their respective communities.

While in England, Kenyatta wrote articles in British newspapers about the desire of Kenyans for independence from England, but he had little success in making his case to British authorities. He returned to Britain two years later, and this time decided to pursue further education. He enrolled at Quaker College, Woodbrooke, and remained there for about a year.

While in England, Kenyatta met and came under the influence of the West Indian intellectual and Pan-Africanist George Padmore. Padmore arranged for Kenyatta to attend Moscow University in the Soviet Union, a communist country. But after Padmore had a falling-out with the Soviets, Kenyatta withdrew from Moscow University and returned to England, where he resumed his studies at University College, London.

Emperor Haile Selassie of Ethiopia visited London in 1936, and Kenyatta broke through a police cordon at the London Railway Station in order to get closer to the little man who was such a big hero to Africans wanting their own independent nations. Two years later, he published a book in Great Britain, *Facing Mount Kenya*, which was a call for independence. Fearing arrest if he were to return to Kenya, he used an alias, Jomo Kenyatta, by which he was known from then on.

In 1945, following the end of World War II, he and other African independence fighters living in England, including Kwame Nkrumah of Gold Coast (present-day Ghana), organized the Fifth Pan-Africanist Congress, adopting the slogans "Freedom Now" and "Africa for Africans." By this time there was great unrest in Kenya, and Kenyatta returned to his native country in the hope of marshalling that unrest in a focused independence movement. Within a few months of his return, he had become president of a new party, Kenya African Union (KAU), and embarked upon a campaign to organize a freedom movement.

The campaign included armed struggle against British rule. Realizing that Kenyatta and his group were becoming increasingly popular, British authorities banned the KAU. In response, the KAU organized landless peasants and low-paid laborers of the Kikuyu tribe into armed bands that attacked government outposts. The groups

A government photo of Jomo Kenyatta, accused by the British of being the "manager" of the secret Mau Mau society.

came to be called Mau Mau, which is probably a corruption of Uma Uma, a Swahili term that means "continually biting." Between 1946 and 1952, the Mau Mau rebellion increased in strength until the British authorities finally declared a state of emergency and arrested Kenyatta and 182 other African leaders.

Brought to trial, Kenyatta was charged with leading the Mau Mau, was convicted, and sentenced to seven years' hard labor and indefinite restrictions thereafter. He served his sentence at Lokitaung in northwestern Kenya and was released in April 1959. He was not allowed to return to Nairobi or to his home territory but was restricted to Lodwar, some ninety miles south of Lokitaung.

The British were unsuccessful in preventing Kenyatta from continuing to influence the Kenya independence movement, however. His followers formed a "Release Jomo Committee." They also formed a new party, the Kenya African National Union (KANU) and elected him president of the party in absentia. Other leaders of the independence movement, including Daniel Arap Moi, visited him at Lodwar and made it clear that they considered him the chief spokesman for their cause.

In August 1961, after nearly two and a half years in internal exile, Kenyatta was released from "house arrest" and allowed to return to his hometown of Gatunda. His followers welcomed him as a returning hero. Later that same year, he led a KANU delegation to London. In May 1963, Kenyans voted for a new, independent government. Kenyatta's KANU party won the majority of the vote, and he became both Prime Minister and Foreign Minister of independent Kenya. June 1, the day Kenya officially became independent, was called Madaraka Day (Swahili for "self-government").

Now that black Africans were in power, white settlers in Kenya were worried. Kenyatta assured them that they would be safe and allowed to live peacefully in the land that they too called home. He urged his fellow black Kenyans to forgive, although never to forget.

On December 12, 1963, Kenya formally became a republic. That same day a son was born to Kenyatta and his wife. He was named Uhuru, which is Swahili for "freedom." One year later, Kenyatta became independent Kenya's first president.

Like the leaders of other newly independent African nations, Kenyatta faced many challenges. He had an economy that had been created to serve the needs of the colonial rulers, not Kenyans. To create a new economy he had to borrow money—often from the same former colonial rulers. He had colonial structures in place—actual buildings as well as systems—that were difficult to change. The most challenging legacy of colonialism was the conglomeration of different tribes that called Kenya home and wanted to direct its future. Intertribal rivalries challenged the country's stability, and there were threats against Kenyatta's life.

Unlike the leaders of other newly independent African nations, Kenyatta managed to avoid major conflicts. On the whole, Kenya saw progress under Kenyatta, who served three terms as president. He still held that office when he died peacefully in his sleep in August 1978.

ALBERT JOHN

LUTHULI

(1898–1967)

T he Zulu chief and religious leader who was the first president of
the African National Congress (ANC), a human rights organization,
was also the first African to be awarded the Nobel Prize for Peace in
recognition of his nonviolent struggle against racial discrimination.

He was born Albert John Mvumbi (Zulu for "Continuous Rain")
Luthuli in Rhodesia. That country, now called Zimbabwe, was then
under the control of Great Britain. His father had moved to Rhodesia
from Zululand in South Africa to work as an interpreter for missionaries. Albert was only ten when his father died. His mother returned
with her children to South Africa, where they were taken in by the
family of his uncle, chief of Groutville, a Zulu community associated
with an American Congregational mission located in the sugar lands
of Natal.

Luthuli's mother paid for his early education by working as a
washerwoman. He then won a scholarship to the American Board of
Missions' teacher-training college at Adams, near Durban. On graduation, he was hired as one of its first three African instructors. In 1927

88

Luthuli married Nokukhanya Bhengu, a teacher and granddaughter of a clan chief.

In 1936 Luthuli left teaching to become the elected chief of the community of five thousand at Groutville. Though confronted by land hunger, poverty, and political voicelessness, he did not yet recognize the need for political action. Even nine years later, when he joined the ANC he was motivated primarily by friendship with its leader. Far more significant to his political awakening was his election to the Natives Representative Council, an advisory body of chiefs and intellectuals set up by the South African government, at the very time when troops and police were brutally crushing a strike of African miners in Witwatersrand, South Africa. This 1946 event cost eight lives and nearly a thousand injuries. Luthuli immediately joined his people's protest against the brutality of the police and regretted that the Natives Representative Council had no power to prevent it. When he toured America in 1948 as a guest of the Congregational Board of Missions, he warned that Christianity faced its severest test in Africa because of racial discrimination. On his return home he found that the Afrikaaner Nationalists had newly come to power. Their National Party, made up primarily of Afrikaaners, the descendants of Dutch settlers in South Africa, had won its first victory in elections on a platform of apartheid, or the complete separation of the races.

At this crucial time, Luthuli was elected president of the Natal African National Congress. Since its founding in 1912, the ANC's efforts to achieve human rights by petitions and mass protests had met with increasing repression. In 1952, stimulated by young black intellectuals, the ANC joined the South African Indian Congress in a countrywide campaign to defy what were deemed unjust laws; eighty-five hundred men and women went voluntarily to prison. As a result of Luthuli's leadership in Natal, the South African government demanded that he resign from the ANC or from his chieftainship. He refused to do either, stating that "the road to freedom is via the cross." The government then deposed him. Not only did he continue to be affectionately regarded as "chief" but also his reputation spread. In that same year, 1952, the ANC elected him president general. Henceforth he was repeatedly banned (under the Suppression of Communism Act, punishment of suspected communist leanings could include confinement to one's home village and denial of attendance at gatherings), but between them he toured the country to address mass meetings.

In December 1956 Luthuli and 155 others were dramatically rounded up and charged with high treason. His long trial failed to prove treason, a communist conspiracy, or violence, and in 1957 he was released. During this time Luthuli's quiet authority and his inspiration to others profoundly impressed distinguished foreign observers, leading to his nomination for the Nobel Peace Prize. Nonwhite people responded in large numbers to his call for a stay-at-home strike in 1957; later, whites also began attending his mass meetings. In 1959 the government again confined him to his rural neighborhood and banned him from gatherings—this time for five years—for "promoting feelings of hostility" between the races.

In the meantime, the National Party government continued to pursue its apartheid policy. In 1953, it instituted Pass Laws requiring black African men to carry an identification card at all times to justify their presence in "white" areas. The Pass Laws were soon extended to women. In 1960, a demonstration against the Pass Laws by residents of Sharpeville, a black suburb of Johannesburg, was put down violently by police. Luthuli called for national mourning, and he himself burned his pass. (He was ill at the time and unable to serve the resulting prison sentence, so he was allowed to pay a fine.) The government outlawed the ANC and its rival offshoot, the Pan-Africanist Congress.

In December 1961 Luthuli was allowed to leave Groutville briefly when he flew with his wife to Oslo, Norway, to receive his Nobel prize. His acceptance address paid tribute to his people's nonviolence and rejection of racism despite adverse treatment, and he noted how far from freedom they remained despite their long struggle.

In fact, many South Africans had concluded that trying to fight the inflexible and cruel apartheid system with nonviolent means was futile. A week after Luthuli's acceptance speech, throughout South Africa, a sabotage group of the ANC called the Spear of the Nation staged several attacks on South African military installations. The policy of nonviolence had at last been abandoned.

Luthuli, back in enforced isolation, could only watch as events in his country continued to unfold. He spent his days working on his autobiography and receiving the few visitors he was permitted by the police. On July 21, 1967, as he crossed a railway bridge near his small farm, Chief Luthuli was struck and killed by a train.

KWAME
NKRUMAH

(1909–1972)

Kwame Nkrumah led the way to the first independent African nation, Ghana. He was born Francis Nwia-Kofi Ngonloma in Nkroful, in the British colony called Gold Coast. That name had been given the region by the Portuguese when they first arrived on the west coast of Africa in the fifteenth century. They found so much gold that they named the place Mina, which means "mine." The fort they built in 1482 for trading in gold, ivory, and slaves is the infamous Elmina Castle of the slave trade.

Nkrumah, the son of a well-to-do goldsmith, attended school in Accra and a Roman Catholic seminary in Amisano. For college, he was sent to the United States. He went to undergraduate school at Lincoln University, an all-black college in Pennsylvania where Langston Hughes, the African-American poet and writer, and Thurgood Marshall, the first African-American U.S. Supreme Court justice, also studied. After receiving his bachelor's degree from Lincoln University in 1939, he did graduate work at the University of Pennsylvania, earning master's degrees in education and philosophy.

Nkrumah then moved to London, where he planned to do further study at the London School of Economics. But a chance meeting changed his plans—and his life. Like Jomo Kenyatta, in London he came under the influence of the West Indian intellectual George Padmore, an organizer of black workers and a member of the Communist Party. Padmore firmly believed in Pan-Africanism, an effort originating among Caribbean intellectuals to unite all people of African heritage around the world and, in particular, those who lived under the yoke of colonialism on the African continent. There had been four earlier Pan-Africanist congresses, the first in 1900. Padmore wanted to organize another in Manchester, England. Nkrumah helped him to do so.

In many ways, the Fifth Pan-Africanist congress was so far the most significant. Several of the delegates, including Nkrumah and Jomo Kenyatta of Kenya, later became leaders of independent African nations, and the conference is regarded as a major step in the movement to decolonize Africa. It marked a significant advance in the participation of workers in the Pan-African cause. It demanded an end to colonial rule and racial discrimination, while it carried forward the broad struggle against imperialism and for human rights and equality of economic opportunity.

Inspired by the conference, Nkrumah joined the West African Students' Union, formed in London in 1925, and soon became vice president, helping to influence that organization's agenda to focus on decolonization of Africa. But he realized he could only do so much from abroad. In 1947, he returned home to join the United Gold Coast Convention, led by Joseph B. Danquah.

Almost immediately, however, Nkrumah realized that he disagreed with both the party's philosophy and its program, which largely ignored the working class. In 1949, he broke with the convention to form the Convention People's Party. Its motto was "Self-government now," and it began a campaign of mass boycotts, strikes, and civil disobedience. For his participation in these actions, Nkrumah was arrested by the British in January 1950.

Pressured by the internal independence movement and international protests, Great Britain agreed to provide for the gradual independence of Gold Coast, which was to be renamed Ghana after the ancient empire of the same name. The new Ghana was five hundred miles south of the ancient kingdom, but historians could trace the movement of the ancient peoples of that kingdom, the Mandinka and Soninke, south to the coast.

In 1951 Nkrumah, while still in prison, ran for and won a seat in the Legislative Assembly; his party won thirty-four out of thirty-eight seats. The British government offered to release him from prison if he in turn agreed to work with them in forming a new government to work toward independence.

That same year Ghana adopted a new constitution, which provided for general elections. Nkrumah's Convention People's Party won two-thirds of the vote. At the age of forty-two, Kwame Nkrumah became president of Ghana. Over the next six years, he presided over a steady movement to full independence. A new constitution in 1954 granted his government broad powers. A popular vote in 1956 in adjacent Togoland, also a British colony, called for union with Ghana. That same year, the Convention People's Party won 68 percent of the seats in the national legislature and passed an independence motion, which the British Parliament approved. In 1957, the British colony of Gold Coast formally became independent Ghana, and three years later a popular vote created the Republic of Ghana, with Nkrumah as prime minister.

Ghana was a charter member of the Organization of African Unity, formed at a conference hosted by Emperor Haile Selassie in Addis Ababa, Ethiopia, in 1963. That same year, Nkrumah published a book titled *Why Africa Must Unite*. But he was unable to devote much time or energy to the cause of Pan-Africanism. He had too many problems in his own country, which he tried both to develop and to unify.

In 1964, even as he pursued development with the completion of the important Akosombo Dam, powerful forces seeking his overthrow, an assassination attempt, and an economic downturn led him to declare Ghana a one-party state and himself Life President (president for life). Two years later, while Nkrumah was in China seeking an aid package and trade negotiations, the army staged a coup and the widely popular National Liberation Party came to power.

Nkrumah never returned to Ghana but instead lived in exile in Guinea. He continued to push for African unity and wrote two more books, *Handbook for Revolutionary Warfare* (1968) and *Class Struggle in Africa* (1970). He died while visiting Romania for medical treatment in April 1972. Celebrated as the father of Ghana's indepencence, Kwame Nkrumah was buried in Ghana.

CONSTANCE
CUMMINGS-JOHN

(1918–2000)

Constance Cummings-John was born Constance Horton in Sierra Leone, then a British colony on the coast of Western sub-Saharan Africa. The area was among the first on the continent to have contact with Europe, and it was one of the first West African British colonies. Still, foreign settlement did not occur until 1787, when it became the first of two colonies established as homes for freed slaves.

By the late eighteenth century, antislavery feelings were running high in the British empire, but few British whites believed that freed slaves could be assimilated into the larger society. So, Great Britain prepared a refuge within its own empire for freed slaves. The town of Freetown was established in Sierra Leone to receive four hundred freedmen from Great Britain, but they were decimated by disease and hostility from the local tribes, primarily Temne and Mende. More freed slaves arrived from Jamaica and other parts of the empire, however, and over time they intermarried with the local people. As the years

passed, the descendants of these returned Africans came to be called Krio (an Africanized form of the word Creole, or mixed people).

In 1821, thirty-four years after Great Britain established its refuge for freed slaves in Sierra Leone, the United States did the same for its freed slaves in Liberia. A group of prominent white Americans formed the American Colonization Society and purchased land north of Sierra Leone to establish Liberia for freed American slaves. In 1847, after only about twenty-five years, Liberia became independent. It would be more than a century before Sierra Leone achieved that goal.

Freetown was the most British of Great Britain's holdings in Africa. In part, that was because the returned Africans had very little in common aside from the British style of life to which they had been exposed. They were originally from all areas of Africa, but they had been cut off from their homes and their own traditions by slavery. In many ways, they were more British than African. Although they never made up more than a small percentage of the colony's population, they dominated the upper classes as well as the area's economy and government. In recognition of that fact, Great Britain divided Sierra Leone into two distinct parts: Freetown, which was a colony dominated by the Krio, and the rest of Sierra Leone, which was a protectorate. During the nineteenth century, the indigenous people of Freetown mounted several unsuccessful revolts against British rule and Krio domination, but these were put down.

Due in no small measure to the presence of the Krio, in the early nineteenth century Freetown was a flourishing trade center. It served as the residence of the British governor who also ruled Gold Coast (now Ghana) and the Gambia settlements. The colony of Sierra Leone soon also became the educational center of British West Africa. Fourah Bay College, established in 1827, was for more than a century the only European-style university in Western sub-Saharan Africa.

When Constance Cummings-John was born in Freetown in 1918, Krios were still the most influential class of Africans. Her family was prominent, and her father was the city's treasurer. She was educated at the top schools for girls in Freetown: Annie Walsh Memorial School, Methodist Girls' High School, and Freetown Secondary School for Girls. Expected to become a teacher, which was considered the appropriate profession for women of her class, she traveled to England at the age of seventeen and enrolled at Whitelands College in Putney, a suburb of London.

In London, like Jomo Kenyatta and Kwame Nkrumah, she was influenced by Pan-Africanism and participated in the activities of two Pan-African organizations, the West African Students' Union (WASU) and the League of Coloured Peoples (LCP). Fired up with a desire for African independence, she determined to return home to teach the less fortunate people of Sierra Leone trades so they could support themselves. She was especially interested in training women for the workplace. Sponsored by the British colonial office, she traveled to the United States to take a six-month course at Cornell University in Ithaca, New York.

It was 1936 and Constance was eighteen years old when she arrived at Cornell, and nothing in her previous experience had prepared her for American racism. If she thought she would find understanding and sympathy from American blacks, she was wrong. They were disdainful of her in their own way, for they failed to understand why she was shocked by the insults and discrimination they had experienced all their lives. Her racial and political consciousness heightened even further, she resolved to double her efforts in the cause of Pan-Africanism. Returning to London, Constance became involved with the International Service Bureau and the Pan-African Federation, which had been founded by Isaac Wallace-Johnson, a fellow anticolonialist from Sierra Leone. Wallace-Johnson, aided by the West Indian pan-Africanist George Padmore, used those organizations to disseminate information to Africans and to get members of the British Parliament interested in the welfare of African workers.

In 1937, Constance married Ethanan Cummings-John, an attorney from Sierra Leone, and the following year the couple returned to their home, determined to fight for independence. Back in Freetown, she was appointed principal of the African Methodist Episcopal Girls' Industrial School, which she found in a dilapidated state and worked to upgrade. Soon, she was also involved in politics. Isaac Wallace-Johnson had returned to Sierra Leone as well, and Constance Cummings-John helped him to organize the West African Youth League. In 1938, at the age of 20, she was elected to the Freetown municipal council.

In September 1939, a few days after England declared war on Germany, Isaac Wallace-Johnson was arrested and thrown into an internment camp along with the German residents of the colony. The charge was criminal libel as a result of a scathing attack on colonialism he had published in August. His arrest put a damper on much of the political activity. Cummings-John continued in her position as a school principal. Her husband was serving in the military, and to support herself she started a quarrying business.

After World War II ended, Cummings-John swallowed her racial pride and tried the United States again. Her husband had died and her fifty-five-year-old half-brother, Asadata Dafora Horton, was making a name for himself in American dance circles performing authentic African dances and creating lavish, full-scale stage productions with African themes. (He had taken the last name Horton because he felt Americans would be more familiar with it than his African name; his great-grandfather had been a slave in Nova Scotia and had taken his owner's name.) Constance Cummings-John stayed with her brother in New York and worked in a New York hospital. She was active in African-American political movements and also worked to raise funds for a school she wanted to open when she returned to Sierra Leone. She came to know the former first lady, Eleanor Roosevelt, who at the time was U.S. Ambassador to the United Nations, and when she did go back to Sierra Leone and open her school, she called it the Eleanor Roosevelt Preparatory School for Girls.

Independence fever was running high in Sierra Leone after the war. By 1951, the British had begun the process of decolonization. A new constitution that year gave power to the peoples of the protectorate, while Krio politicians founded their own party. Constance Cummings-John was among the younger Krio intellectuals who understood that Sierra Leone could never prosper with such a divided population. Rather than join the Krio politicians, she joined the Sierra Leone Peoples Party (SLPP), which had been established by the politicians in the protectorate. This move angered many of her fellow Krios. In the meantime, she again won a seat on Freetown's city council, where she became known as a champion of Freetown's market women. In 1952, she founded the Sierra Leone Women's Movement, establishing branches in both the colony and the protectorate, creating a women's trading cooperative, educational and welfare projects, and also a newspaper.

In 1957, she ran for national office and was elected to the house of representatives, but her old Krio enemies banded together and forced her resignation. In 1962, following Sierra Leone's independence from Great Britain, she campaigned for a seat in the house of representatives again, but she allied herself with what turned out to be a losing faction of the SLPP and was defeated. Four years later, she campaigned for and won the mayoralty of Freetown, becoming the first woman ever to serve as mayor of a major city in Africa.

In 1967, she happened to be at a conference outside the country when a military coup dissolved the nation's government, including the Freetown City Council. She did not return home. Instead, she settled in a suburb of London, where she became active in Labor Party politics and worked in the disarmament movement. After a nine-year exile, considering her native country stable enough for her to return, she went back home and took up her work with the Sierra Leone

Women's Movement. But political conditions soon deteriorated and she went back to London, watching with anguish from afar as the government changed hands again and again and ethnic and political enmities brought ruin to her country, which remains one of the poorest in Africa.

In 1996, Constance Cummings-John published her autobiography, *Memoirs of a Krio Leader*, in which she wrote proudly of her work with women and education and somewhat ruefully about her career in politics. Her major fault, she said, was assuming that her own loyalty, generosity, and courage were shared by the male politicians who had managed to ruin her beloved country.

N E L S O N
MANDELA

(B. 1918)

T he man who is most credited with bringing down the hated system of apartheid (the Afrikaans word for "separateness" of the races) in South Africa was born on July 18, 1918, in a village in the Transkei. His father was the principal advisor to the acting paramount chief of Thembuland, and the young Nelson Rolihlahla Mandela grew up in comparative privilege. He was educated at a local mission school and continued his education at home, where he grew up hearing stories from the elders of his tribe about their ancestors' resistance to European encroachment on their land.

After his father died, the young Nelson Mandela became a ward of the paramount chief. Trained to assume high office when he was grown, he became interested in the legal cases that came before the chief's court and determined instead to become a lawyer. He attended secondary school at Healdtown, then enrolled at the University College of Fort Hare. He showed strong leadership qualities and was elected to the Students' Representative Council, but he failed to graduate because he was suspended for his participation in a protest boycott.

Mandela then went to Johannesburg, where he got a job as a clerk in an attorney's office. He completed his bachelor's degree by taking correspondence courses, then began to study for his law degree. He continued his political activity by joining the African National Congress in 1942. The ANC had been formed in 1912 as the South African Native National Congress. It was created to oppose the passage of the 1913 Natives' Land Act, which froze existing "tribal" areas and stopped native Africans from acquiring land outside those areas. The South African Native National Congress then fought against laws requiring blacks to carry identification passes when they were in white areas. Changing its name to the African National Congress in 1923, the organization continued to defend the rights of the black majority in South Africa. Although it was well respected among black South Africans, the ANC had mostly professionals as members and had confined itself to legal challenges and polite petitioning of the government. It had made little headway against the entrenched racism of South Africa's rulers.

World War II had broken out in Europe in the late 1930s and eventually affected North Africa. As European countries fought one another, eventually joined by Asian countries such as Japan and China and by the United States, a wave of nationalist feeling swept Africa. Younger members of the ANC like Mandela were inspired by African nationalism and believed that the ANC should expand both its membership base and its operations and push more strongly for national self-determination. In 1944, Mandela was part of a group of young men, all living around the Witwatersrand area of Johannesburg, who decided to transform the ANC into a mass movement. Led by Anton Lembede, this group also included Walter Sisulu and Oliver Tambo. That year they formed the ANC Youth League (ANCYL), whose purpose was to reach out to the millions of uneducated working people in the towns and the peasants in the countryside. That same year, Mandela also married Evelyn Ntoko Mase.

The ANC Youth League worked to increase membership at the grassroots level and also to persuade members of the ANC that their more activist stance was the way of the future. At the 1945 ANC annual conference, two members of the Youth League were elected to the organization's executive committee. Because of Mandela's leadership qualities he was made the head of the Youth League in 1947.

The following year, in an all-white election, the National Party, which had campaigned on a platform of apartheid, came to power. The election of a government committed to the degradation of black South Africans galvanized the ANCYL. Its leaders, including Nelson Mandela, Oliver Tambo, and Walter Sisulu, drew up a "Program of Action" that aimed to achieve full citizenship. It included redistribution of the land, trade union rights, free education for all children and adults, and respect for the various black South African cultures. The ultimate aim was an end to apartheid and full political representation for all South Africans. At the 1949 ANC conference, the leaders of the Youth League exercised their growing influence to oust the more conservative leaders of the ANC and replace them with younger, more activist leaders. Walter Sisulu was elected secretary-general. The following year, Nelson Mandela was elected to the ANC executive committee. The ANC adopted the Program of Action that had been crafted by the leaders of the Youth League, which called for more militant tactics, such as boycotts, strikes, and other forms of civil disobedience and noncooperation with the government's policies.

The national government paid no attention, and went about implementing its apartheid policies. Eventually, those policies included requiring first nonwhite men and then nonwhite women to carry identity cards and restricted blacks to defined, nonwhite areas; reorganizing the education system so that fewer black children could go to school; and generally reducing the rights of the huge black majority.

Organizing to fight apartheid in 1952, the ANC instituted the Campaign for the Defiance of Unjust Laws, with Nelson Mandela as national volunteer-in-chief of a mass civil disobedience campaign. It would grow from a small core of selected volunteers to involve more and more ordinary people who would defy the apartheid laws, fill the jails, and overwhelm the whites-only system. Mandela traveled around the country, organizing the small groups of volunteers, and was soon arrested on charges of fomenting violence and encouraging communism. At the trial of Mandela and several others, the government was unable to prove that they had advised a course other than peaceful action. But Mandela was convicted of encouraging communism, given a suspended sentence, and put under restriction—prohibited from attending gatherings and forbidden to leave Johannesburg for six months.

In recognition of his work in the defiance campaign, Mandela was elected to the presidency of the ANC Youth League. He was also elected president of the Transvaal chapter of the ANC, one that was so important in the organization that he automatically became deputy president of the entire ANC.

While under restriction, Mandela studied for and passed the attorney's examination and was admitted to the practice of law. He opened an office in Johannesburg with Oliver Tambo. Their law practice focused on assisting black South Africans in fighting for their rights against apartheid—peasants ejected from land that had been worked by their families for generations, people arrested for being in a white area without a pass from a white person. Every morning, when Mandela and Tambo arrived at work, long lines of impoverished, humiliated black South Africans awaited them, and they worked night and day to get justice for their people.

During this period, Mandela's first marriage ended in divorce and he married a young medical social worker named Winnie Madikizela. Some twenty years younger than her husband, she had been born in the Transkei and had become politically active after relocating to Johannesburg. She married Mandela knowing that his first allegiance was to the cause of equal rights for black South Africans.

The legal efforts of Mandela and Tambo did not sit well with the authorities, who tried to force them to move their practice miles away from Johannesburg. They also tried to bar Mandela from practicing law because of his conviction in court. He successfully fought to maintain his office and keep up his practice. But as time went by, more and more policies were enacted to separate the races and confine blacks to specific "homeland" areas, to deny education to black children, and to deprive blacks of nearly every right they had. Mandela realized that the ANC must decentralize. He devised what came to be called the M-plan, named for him, by which local chapters of the ANC would be strengthened so they could carry out their work in the absence of strong central leadership.

For most of the 1950s, Mandela and other ANC leaders were arrested, put under restrictions, and imprisoned. During the latter part of the decade, he was among the accused in the mass Treason Trial, by which the government aimed to weaken the ANC leadership.

In March 1960, the Pan-Africanist Congress organized a protest against apartheid—particularly the Pass Laws—in the black suburb of Johannesburg called Sharpeville. They prevented the bus drivers from going on duty, so that there were no buses to take people to work, and led a crowd to protest in front of the municipal building. An estimated five thousand to seven thousand were in attendance. Rarely had so many black people demonstrated their defiance of the apartheid laws in any way. Police attempted to disperse the crowd, and some in the crowd threw stones at them. A melee resulted, with police setting off tear-gas bombs and charging the crowd with their batons and the crowd responding with stones and, according to some reports, gunfire. In the end, sixty-nine protesters were killed and one hundred eighty were wounded in what came to be known as the Sharpeville Massacre.

After the Sharpeville Massacre, the government outlawed the Pan-Africanist Congress and the ANC. Mandela and other leaders of these organizations were detained. But the Sharpeville Massacre had made them even more determined to fight the government. In March 1961, the

ANC convened an All-in African Conference in Pietermaritzburg that attracted fourteen hundred delegates, all of whom risked their freedom by attending in defiance of the government's efforts to stamp out protest. At the time, South Africa was moving toward independence from Great Britain. In a memorable keynote speech, Mandela challenged the interim government to organize a national convention at which representatives of all South Africans could have a voice in writing a new, democratic constitution. If the government persisted in denying basic rights to non-white South Africans, he warned, it faced a mass general strike.

Because his speech was treasonous, Mandela then went underground to lead the general strike. He was somewhat disappointed that more black South Africans did not engage in the protest, but heartened that at least some were not too afraid of government reprisals to support the strike. In response, the interim government mobilized the military, and the independent Republic of South Africa was born in an atmosphere of unrest and fear.

Nelson Mandela operated for approximately a year while living underground, moving from place to place and disguising himself as a laborer or a chauffeur to avoid detection by South African authorities. He rarely saw his wife and children. By early June 1961, he and other ANC leaders had concluded that it was unrealistic to continue trying to oppose the government by nonviolent means. Under Mandela's leadership, a separate, radical arm of the ANC was formed. Umkhonto we Sizwe, which means Spear of the Nation, would engage in guerrilla warfare against the government. Wrote Mandela some years later, "It was only when all else had failed, when all channels of peaceful protest had been barred to us, that the decision was made to embark on violent forms of political struggle, and to form Umkhonto we Sizwe . . . the Government had left us no other choice."

While he arranged for guerrilla training for members of that new, armed wing of the ANC, Mandela left the country in 1962 and traveled abroad for several months, attracting political and financial support.

He spoke at the Conference of the Pan African Freedom Movement of East and Central Africa in Ethiopia and visited the heads of state of several newly independent African nations. Not long after his return to South Africa he was arrested. Charged with a number of offenses, including illegally leaving the country, incitement to strike, and sabotage, he used his trial as a platform to air his views. He believed that not only he was on trial but also the hopes and dreams of the South African people, and he decided to act as his own attorney.

At the trial, he charged that he was not bound to obey the laws of a white parliament in which he was not represented, and that a trial by a legal system controlled by whites could not be a fair one. His self-defense was a defense of the will to achieve freedom and justice:

> I have fought against white domination, and I have fought against black domination. I have cherished the ideal of a democratic and free society in which all persons live together in harmony and with equal opportunities. It is an ideal which I hope to live for and to achieve. But if needs be, it is an ideal for which I am prepared to die.

Sentenced to life imprisonment in 1964, he spent twenty-two years in a maximum security prison on Robben Island off the coast of Cape Town. His wife Winnie was prevented from traveling and attending group events. Although unable to actively pursue equality for black South Africans, the imprisoned Mandela remained a potent symbol of the injustice of apartheid. Over time, the rest of the world increasingly isolated South Africa economically, socially, and morally. Several times the government tried to bargain with Mandela, offering him freedom if he would accept its policies. Each time he steadfastly refused. Eventually, even most white South Africans realized the apartheid system could not work any longer. They voted in a new, more liberal government, which moved Mandela to a minimum security prison and finally released him in February 1990 after twenty-six

After his release from prison, Nelson Mandela raises his fist as he speaks to a crowded stadium in Soweto.

years behind bars. He walked out of prison an international hero.

In 1991, at the first national conference of the ANC held inside South Africa in more than thirty years, Mandela was elected president of the organization. In that role, he undertook negotiations with the government that eventually yielded the first free elections in South Africa. In 1993, he accepted the Nobel Peace Prize, the highest international award, on behalf of all South Africans who had suffered and sacrificed to bring peace and justice to their land. In 1994, Nelson Mandela became the president of South Africa.

More disappointment awaited him, however. He and his wife Winnie had become strangers during their long years of separation. Banned, exiled, and frequently imprisoned, she was subjected to as much humiliation as the government could impose. She had become embittered and determined to reap the benefits of her new status. Winnie Mandela was charged with a number of offenses, including fraud and collusion in the death of a former aide. Nelson Mandela divorced her in 1996. In July 2004, she was convicted of forty-three counts of fraud and given a five-year suspended prison sentence. Ordinary Africans remained loyal to her, however, and she continued as head of the ANC Women's League.

In 1998, on his eightieth birthday, Nelson Mandela married Graca Machel, widow of Samora Machel, the former Mozambican president and ANC ally who had been killed in an air crash fifteen years earlier. The following year, he stepped down as president of South Africa. He retired from public life and returned to his birthplace, Qunu, Transkei, as one of the most respected human beings on earth.

ALBERTINA
SISULU

(B. 1918)

The woman who became known as the "Mother of a Nation" among South Africans opposed to apartheid was born as Nontsikelelo Thethiwe in Cofimvaba in the Transkei, on October 21, 1918. She was the second of five children. When young Nontsikelelo enrolled at the local primary school run by Presbyterian missionaries, she was given a list of Christian names from which to choose. She chose Albertina and was baptized in her new name. When both her parents died, the children were separated and sent to live with various relatives. Albertina was taken in by her mother's family. Educated at Catholic mission schools, her first ambition was to be a nun. But after she found out she would have to give up contact with her brothers and sisters, she changed her mind. Her fond dream as a child was to set up a home where she and her siblings could be together.

Albertina decided to be a nurse instead. In 1939, after completing elementary and secondary school, she was accepted into the nurse-training program at a hospital in Johannesburg, the largest city in South Africa. During her training, she met Walter Sisulu, the brother

115

of a fellow nurse. Sisulu was already deeply involved in the work of the African National Congress. In 1944, with Nelson Mandela, Oliver Tambo, and others, he formed the ANC Youth League, which brought new energy and commitment to the organization's goal of nonviolent mass action against the legal underpinnings of white supremacy.

Albertina had not been particularly interested in politics, but after she met Walter, she was inspired to fight against apartheid and for a free South Africa. She and Walter were married in 1944, the same year she qualified as a nurse and midwife, and the same year as the formation of the ANC Youth League. She, too, became a member.

In 1948, in elections in which mostly whites were able to vote, the Afrikaner-led National Party gained control of the government and quickly went about installing a policy of apartheid. The ANC stepped up its activities and its membership increased greatly, making it necessary to elect officers who could work in the cause full time. Walter Sisulu was the favorite candidate for secretary-general of the ANC, and Albertina agreed to support them both so he could devote all his time to ANC work.

She also kept up her own political activity in the ANC Women's League. In 1954, she became a member of the executive committee of the Federation of South African Women, a new organization that she helped to form, in part, to protest the Bantu Education Act. The previous year the South African government had passed the legislation that had a severe effect on the education of black South African children. Prior to that time, 90 percent of black children had been educated by state-aided mission schools.

The term "Bantu" was used by white South Africans to refer to all black South Africans, although it is actually the name of an African language. The Bantu Act required that all such schools register with the state and removed control of African education from the churches and local authorities. A new policy centralized the education of black children in the government's Bantu Education Department, which was dedicated to keeping black education separate and inferior. The Roman Catholic Church was largely alone in its attempt to keep its schools going without state aid. The 1953 law also separated the financing of education for black Africans from general state spending and linked it directly to taxes paid by Africans themselves. As a result, far less was spent on black children than on white children. Albertina Sisulu was a leader in the boycott of the Bantu Education Act. For some time she conducted classes for black children in her own home.

Not long afterward, the National Party government instituted the Pass Laws, requiring black African men to carry an identification card at all times to justify their presence in "white" areas. When the Pass Laws were extended to women, Albertina Sisulu was one of the leaders of a demonstration of twenty thousand women in Pretoria, capital of South Africa, in 1956. Two years later, she was among the leaders of a similar demonstration in Johannesburg. She was arrested and jailed for three weeks, a wrenching experience because it meant being separated from her three sons and her ten-month-old daughter, Nonkululeko (Freedom). It did not dissuade her from the freedom struggle, however. In fact, she increased her political activity, becoming treasurer of the ANC Women's League in 1959.

The ANC's opposition to the Pass Laws continued. In fact, it increased greatly as black South African dissatisfaction with apartheid grew, fueled by the growing number of newly independent nations in Africa and by the achievements against segregation of the civil rights movement in the United States. In March 1960, a huge demonstration against the laws in the black suburb of Johannesburg called Sharpeville resulted in sixty-nine protesters being shot and killed and many more wounded by South African police. The South African government then banned the ANC and another group, the Pan-Africanist Congress, from further political activity. The South African Congress of Trade Unions, which was sympathetic to the work of both groups, was soon also driven underground.

Persuaded that nonviolent means of protest were not going to work against the Afrikaner determination to separate and marginalize the black African majority, ANC leaders came to the conclusion that armed means had become a legitimate form of resistance. In 1961, they created Umkhonto we Sizwe (Spear of the Nation) to carry out armed attacks against the government. One year later, South African authorities arrested its commander, Nelson Mandela. Walter Sisulu and other ANC leaders were forced to go underground.

On June 29, 1963, Walter Sisulu began to broadcast from exile over a station the ANC called Radio Freedom, calling for ANC supporters to fight back against the apartheid authorities. In an attempt to trace the origin of the broadcast, South African police detained Albertina Sisulu. Held in solitary confinement for seven weeks, she was released unbowed, and immediately led demonstrations against repression and the trials of the leaders of the freedom movement.

Walter Sisulu and Nelson Mandela were captured and sentenced to life imprisonment in 1964. Their wives, Albertina Sisulu and Winnie Mandela, were served with harsh five-year banning orders that prohibited them from attending any gatherings of more than two persons (which meant they could not even attend church), confining them to their hometowns, and preventing them from engaging in any political activities.

Albertina had to struggle to support her family, which came to include not only her own three sons and daughter but also a niece and nephew whom she took in after their parents died. She continued to work as a nurse and earned extra money by knitting at home. In 1969, when the first five-year banning order elapsed, she was served with a second five-year order, this one confining her to her home on nights and weekends. A third five-year banning order confined her to her home even on public holidays.

In 1979, she received a two-year banning order, without house arrest and with permission to go to church. When the two years had elapsed, during a brief time when she was not under ban, she accepted as many invitations to speak at meetings all over the country as she could, although, as a person once banned, she could not be quoted in newspapers. She was also an honored guest at a conference of political, trade union, and community organizations in Durban in 1981. Banned again from June 1982 to July 1983, she was free the following month to attend the funeral of a woman leader of the movement. Because she joined in the singing of ANC songs at the funeral she was arrested, tried, and convicted. Sentenced to four years in prison, she was released on bail pending appeal.

By this time, the apartheid regime of the Republic of South Africa had become increasingly isolated by the rest of the world. Most democratic nations refused to do business with the country and repeatedly called for reforms that would give a voice to its majority nonwhite residents. In response to the continuing international pressure, and to the continuing unrest within its own borders, the new government of F. W. de Klerk introduced a new constitution in 1984. It established a stratified hierarchy that recognized 25 percent of the population as citizens: whites, coloreds (those of mixed race), and East Indians were each to have their own house of parliament. The 75 percent of the population that was black, however, a total of twenty million people, were not recognized as citizens and were given no representation.

Needless to say, that new constitution only fanned the flames of discontent. When it was still in the proposal stage, a group of major antiapartheid organizations banned together and formed the United Democratic Front (UDF), which staged demonstrations against the proposed new constitution and, after that constitution was implemented, for its repeal. Soon after her release, Albertina Sisulu led a mass mobilization by the UDF against the government's new racist constitution and other apartheid measures. Detained with other leaders of the UDF in December 1984 on a charge of high treason, she again spent several months in jail before the case was dismissed on appeal. In February 1988 she was prohibited anew from engaging in all political activity.

Meanwhile, her children had followed their parents into anti-apartheid activity, as had the niece and nephew whom she had raised. Her eldest son, Vuyisile Max, had been detained with his mother after his father's 1963 Radio Freedom broadcast. Harassed by the police after his release from prison, he left the country. A daughter, Lindiwe, was detained for eleven months after protests in 1976 and later went into exile. Another son, Mlungisi, and her niece and nephew were all detained after protesting the racist 1984 constitution. Her youngest son, Zwelakhe, editor of an antiapartheid newspaper, *New Nation*, had been restricted and jailed several times, and he was held in detention for more than two years for his work against the 1984 constitution.

At last, the white leaders of South Africa realized they could not continue the policies of apartheid in the face of such determined internal opposition—not to mention the international moral and economic sanctions. In 1990, a new government under President P. W. Botha removed the ban on the ANC and the UFD, released Walter Sisulu and Nelson Mandela after twenty-six years in prison, and organized new elections. In April 1994, the ANC won a landslide victory in the country's first real democratic election in which Nelson Mandela was elected president, Walter Sisulu vice president, and Albertina Sisulu a member of Parliament.

Well into her eighties, Albertina Sisulu has continued to work as a member of Parliament, as an ANC leader in her home area of Soweto, outside Johannesburg, and as president of the World Peace Council. Revered as the Mother of the Movement, she once said, "Although politics has given me a rough life, there is absolutely nothing I regret about what I have done and what has happened to me and my family throughout all these years. Instead, I have been strengthened and feel more of a woman than I would otherwise have felt if my life was different."

SIR SERETSE
KHAMA

(1921–1980)

Among the British colonial territories in southern Africa was Bechuanaland. Located above South Africa, it was a thinly populated, mostly desert area. Seretse Khama, who would lead it into independence as Botswana, was born in 1921 in the town of Serowe in the east-central part of the territory, then called the Bamangwato Reserve. Named for the tribe that populated it, the Bamangwato Reserve comprised an area of approximately forty thousand square miles and had been established in 1899 in the time of Seretse's grandfather, Khama III. Seretse's father, Sekgoma, was chief of the Bamangwato. There was a memorial in Serowe to Khama III. Located in a fertile, well-watered area, the town was a trade and commerce center that had produced many leaders of the Bamangwato people.

Seretse means "the clay that binds together," and the child Seretse was a living symbol of the reconciliation between his grandfather and father. Khama III had chosen Seretse's mother as his son Sekgoma's new wife. Khama III died in 1923. When Sekgoma died in 1925, four-year-old Seretse was proclaimed king. Because he was too young to

rule, his uncle Tshekedi Khama became regent and later sole guardian of Seretse.

Seretse was a sickly child, but he grew into a healthy adolescent. He attended boarding schools and college in South Africa. In 1945, his uncle sent him to England to study law. Two years later, while in London pursuing his legal studies, Seretse Khama met a young Englishwoman his age named Ruth Williams. The daughter of a retired officer in the British army in India, Ruth had served in the Women's Auxiliary Air Force during World War II and was working as a clerk for the British insurance company Lloyd's of London. The two met at a London Missionary Society dance and were not initially attracted to one another. But they both loved jazz music, and that shared enthusiasm eventually resulted in romance. By September 1948 they had decided to get married.

Such a marriage was highly unusual in those days, and the young couple had to overcome a number of barriers in order to wed. Their families were opposed to the marriage. Ruth's father refused to accept it, and the two stopped speaking. Her employer told her that if she married Seretse she would either have to quit Lloyd's of London altogether or transfer to the company's office in New York, where interracial marriage was more acceptable. Seretse's uncle back in Bechuanaland, informed of his nephew's plans by airmail letter, pressed officials of the London Missionary Society to intervene. The vicar (minister) of a London church was afraid to conduct the marriage ceremony and referred the young couple to the Bishop of London. The bishop refused to allow the marriage to take place in the church without the approval of the British government. The couple knew that was unlikely to be granted, so they got married in a civil ceremony at the Kensington Registry Office.

Scandalized, Tshekedi Khama ordered his nephew home. At a full tribal assembly in late October, Seretse was strongly criticized for breaking with tribal custom, his marriage was condemned, and tribal authorities resolved to prevent his wife from entering the Bamangwato Reserve. Seretse refused to budge, and after a time some of the tribal authorities came around to his way of thinking. They also began to suspect that Seretse's uncle was less concerned about tribal custom than he was about banishing Seretse and becoming chief himself. In December, at a second full assembly, a number of people withdrew their objections to the marriage. Seretse returned to his new wife and his legal studies in London. In June 1949, having earned his law degree, he went back to Bechuanaland. He made it clear that if his wife was not allowed to join him, he would leave permanently. A third full tribal assembly agreed to accept him as their chief on any terms. Ruth Williams Khama arrived in Serowe in August. Tshekedi Khama, who as regent had ruled over the tribe for twenty years, went into exile with a small group of loyal followers.

Seretse Khama's troubles were far from over. The British government refused to recognize him as chief. South Africa declared him and his wife "prohibited immigrants." Much more than interracial marriage was at issue. It had only been a year since the National Party in South Africa (made up primarily of Afrikaaners, the descendants of Dutch settlers in South Africa) had won its first victory in the 1948 elections on a platform of apartheid, or complete separation of the races. In neighboring Southern Rhodesia, where the National Party was also strong, the prime minister told the British that the more extreme nationalists would not be willing to remain associated with a country that officially recognized an African chief married to a white woman. In fact, he feared that the nationalists might take the occasion to push for the establishment of a republic outside the British Commonwealth—or even make armed attack on Bechuanaland. The last thing the British needed was turmoil in southern Africa or any disruption in South Africa's production of gold and uranium.

The British government was in a dilemma. If it tried to influence Seretse Khama, it would be accused of racism and pandering to white opinion in South Africa. On the other hand, if it did nothing, it might not be able to ensure the safety of Bechuanaland and the Bamangwato. The government decided to conduct an inquiry in order to buy time and allow tempers to cool. The inquiry's purpose was to assess the suitability of Seretse Khama for the chieftainship of the Bamangwato. The judge appointed to conduct the inquiry reported to the government in December 1949 that Seretse was eminently fit to rule. But that was not what the British government wanted to hear. The judge's report was suppressed, and the government declared that while Seretse himself was fit to lead his people and they had accepted his marriage, having a wife who was white would prevent friendly and cooperative relations with South Africa and Rhodesia. Since such relations were essential to the well-being of the Bamangwato and to Bechuanaland, Seretse could not be deemed fit to rule.

In 1950, Seretse returned to London to continue with his law studies. His wife was pregnant with their first child by this time and remained in Bechuanaland, where Seretse was permitted to return to be present at the birth. The family went back to London as soon as Ruth and the baby could travel. By this time her father had had a change of heart and welcomed them. Meanwhile, Seretse's uncle Tshekedi was also banned from the Bamangwato Reserve while the British arranged for a caretaker government.

Sir Seretse Khama with his wife, Ruth, and their two children in the garden of their Croydon home.

The treatment of Seretse and Ruth Khama by the British government caused international outrage. In London, Khama had the support of many influential people. Back in Bechuanaland, his people also continued to agitate for his return. In 1956, the Bamangwato sent a cable to the British Queen Elizabeth, asking for the return of their chief. The new British Commonwealth relations minister realized that Britain had to distance itself from the racism of South Africa. But it was still too politically dangerous to allow Khama to be chief of Bechuanaland, so a compromise was worked out. After both Seretse and Tshekedi signed an agreement renouncing the chieftainship for themselves and agreeing to live in harmony, both were allowed to return home as private citizens.

Back home, Seretse became a cattle rancher and entered local politics. He founded the Bechuanaland Democratic Party, which swept aside its Pan-Africanist and socialist rivals to win the 1965 elections, the prelude to his country's gaining independence as Botswana in 1966. Seretse Khama became prime minister and then, on September 30, 1966, president of the Republic of Botswana. That same year Queen Elizabeth knighted him, and he became Sir Seretse Khama.

A soft-spoken, gentle man, Sir Seretse Khama came to office with great moral authority. He had proved that he was willing to risk his power for the woman he loved, and his people had never forgotten that. Like many other leaders of newly independent African nations, he inherited an impoverished state. In fact, Botswana was believed to be the poorest country in Africa. Unlike many African leaders, he did not have to constantly fight enemies to stay in power. He could concentrate on pursuing economic and governmental policies that would produce a stable nation and a contented people. It helped, of course, that Botswana had productive diamond mines—it became the world's largest producer of gem diamonds—but other African countries have had abundant natural resources and still proved economically unstable. Under Sir Seretse Khama, Botswana's beef processing and gold-and-diamond mining formed the basis of an export-oriented economy. Profits from that economy were used to build roads, schools, and hospitals. General prosperity increased.

Having stabilized his country's economy, Sir Seretse turned his attention beyond its borders. He was one of the "Front-Line Presidents" in a region that was embroiled in civil war, racial enmity, and corruption. Sir Seretse was able to envision a southern Africa after colonialism and apartheid. He helped move forward the peaceful transfers of the British colony of Rhodesia and the German colony of South-West Africa to black self-rule as the independent nations of Zimbabwe and Namibia, respectively.

Sir Seretse Khama died in 1980 at the age of fifty-nine, of complications from diabetes that had been first diagnosed twenty years earlier. Only after his death did the report written by the British judge in 1949 come to light—the report that had found Sir Seretse fit to rule. His widow, known popularly as Lady K, continued to live in Botswana, where she did a great deal of charity work and served for a time as president of the Botswana Red Cross. She died in 2002, survived by their four children, a daughter and three sons, one of whom became vice president of Botswana.

JULIUS
NYERERE
(1922–1999)

J ulius Nyerere presided over the creation of the nation of Tanzania from two former British colonies, Tanganyika and Zanzibar. One of the most respected leaders of the African independence movements, he was called Mwalimu, which means teacher.

He was born Julius Kambarage Nyerere on April 13, 1922, in Butiama, on the eastern shore of Lake Victoria in northwest Tanganyika. His father was the chief of the small Zanaki tribe in a region so rural that the nearest school was twenty-six miles away. As a result, Nyerere did not begin his education until he was twelve years old. He did well in school and continued on to a government secondary school operated by Roman Catholic missionaries. On graduation, he attended Makerere University in Kampala, Uganda, where he earned a teaching certificate.

Nyerere then took a teaching position, but he was so obviously bright and ambitious that he won a singular honor as the first Tanganyikan youth to win a government scholarship to a university in Great Britain. He studied history and political economy at the

University of Edinburgh in Scotland, earning a master's degree and becoming only the second Tanganyikan to achieve a university degree outside Africa.

While at Edinburgh, Nyerere encountered socialism, an economic system in which the means of production, distribution, and exchange are owned by the community collectively, usually through the government. It is distinguished from capitalism, the predominant economic system in Europe and the United States, which is characterized by individual wealth and competitive economic activity. Nyerere saw parallels between socialism and traditional African communal living. He believed that a socialist form of government would be best for his people.

As elsewhere in Africa after World War II, Tanganyikans were campaigning for independence. On his return to his homeland, Nyerere again worked as a teacher; but he was as keen for independence as other young Tanganyikans and found himself engaging in political work as well. In fact, he was soon forced by the colonial authorities to choose between the two activities. They did not want teachers who were engaged in politics. Reluctantly, Nyerere, who loved teaching, chose to forego it in order to work for his country's freedom.

A number of different political parties were campaigning for independence. Nyerere could see the value of all of them but realized they would be better off working together than separately. He devoted himself to uniting the parties to work for their common goal. Slight of build, with a quiet sense of humor, Nyerere was a fine speaker and a skilled organizer. He was also a consensus builder, and in 1954 he achieved his goal with the formation of the Tanganyika African National Union (TANU). He was elected its president. Four years later, he won election to the colonial legislative council, and two years after that he was made chief minister.

Fortunately for Tanganyika, the British governor, Sir Richard Turnbull, respected Nyerere and helped him all he could. The mechanisms for Tanganyikan self-rule were put into place without bloodshed. In 1961, the British colonial authorities granted Tanganyika internal self-government. Nyerere became premier. He presided over the writing of a new constitution, and Tanganyika won full independence in December 1961. In elections the following year, he became president of the new nation.

As well-respected as Nyerere was, he still had enemies and adversaries who sought the power he possessed. Early on, an attempt was made to overthrow him. A similar event in neighboring Zanzibar, also newly independent, led Nyerere to negotiate with the new leaders in Zanzibar to unite the two countries. The name chosen for the combined nation, the Republic of Tanzania, also combined the two names Tanganyika and Zanzibar.

As president, Nyerere had to steer a difficult course. By the late 1960s Tanzania was one of the world's poorest countries. It had a few diamond mines and some agricultural exports—including a small coffee-growing region—but not much else in the way of an economy. Not one of the roads that connected the northern and southern regions was passable in all types of weather. Like many other newly independent African nations, Tanzania carried a huge foreign debt and suffered a decrease in foreign aid as its economic troubles mounted. Even the price of the agricultural products Tanzania exported fell.

Nyerere's solution to his country's economic problems was based on the ideas he had as a college student in Scotland about combining socialism with traditional communal living. His government nationalized, or took control of, most of the private industry in the country. He also organized agricultural production around villages so that each village was responsible for the production of the crops in its area. The idea was to extend traditional values and responsibilities around kinship to Tanzania as a whole.

Although it was a good theory, Nyerere's solution did not work very well in reality. One major problem was the country's lack of basic resources. Another was that many people resisted the idea of being reorganized, moved, and having their land taken from them. Productivity went down.

Nyerere's ideas about self-reliance were more successful when applied to health care and education. He made both services available to more people. In school curricula, he emphasized pride in Tanzanian languages and traditions. He also tried to further his ideal of economic equality. When he felt that the members of his government—all from his TANU party—had become out of touch with the poor people, he ordered them to walk two hundred miles to a party convention, passing through and spending the night in peasant villages.

Outside forces prevented Nyerere from creating the self-sustaining independent nation he had dreamed about for so long. The legacy of colonialism, tribal warfare in neighboring countries, and world economic forces beyond his control were among them. So was divisiveness in his own country. When Nyerere feared that his opponents were threatening his plans to stabilize his country, he ordered them imprisoned. He also kept Tanzania a one-party state, denying his opponents the opportunity to run against him and his party in free elections.

In 1985, when he was in his early sixties, Nyerere gave up the presidency but remained chairman of the TANU Party, which ran Tanzania. Five years later, he gave up that position as well. He remained active in African affairs, especially in the work of the Organization of African Unity, which he had helped found. In 1996, he served as chief mediator in the civil war in neighboring Burundi. He died of leukemia on October 14, 1999.

KENNETH
KAUNDA

(B . 1 9 2 4)

Kenneth Kaunda fought for the independence of Zambia, which shares a border with Tanzania, and became its first president. He was born on April 28, 1924, of Bantu-speaking people at Lubwa Mission when Zambia was the British colony of Northern Rhodesia. The colony had been named for Cecil John Rhodes, the British diamond tycoon who had sought expansion of the British Empire in southern Africa.

Kenneth was one of eight children. His father was the Reverend David Kaunda, an ordained Church of Scotland missionary and teacher. His mother was one of the first women teachers in the country. Kenneth received his elementary education at the mission school, and during those years he also learned how to play the guitar. Throughout his life, he rarely went anywhere without his guitar. After more studies at a secondary school in Lusaka, the capital of Northern Rhodesia, he earned a teaching certificate and returned home in 1943 to take up a job at the mission school at Chinsali Mission. Within a year he was named headmaster. That he was only twenty years old

at the time indicates that he had strong leadership qualities. It also attests to the limited number of qualified teachers in the colony.

World War II had broken out in 1939. Although southern Africa was not directly affected by the fighting, the war gave rise to new political movements that grew and flourished after the war ended in 1945. Kaunda joined the Chinsali Young Men's Farming Association, leaving his post as headmaster of the Chinsali Mission School when he was voted its secretary in 1947. As Julius Nyerere had also learned, British colonial authorities frowned on teachers engaging in political activity. In 1948, Kaunda worked briefly as a welfare officer for the Chingola copper mine but returned to teaching later in the year after the authorities rethought their decision.

At the end of the 1940s, Great Britain was intent on combining some of its colonies in southern Africa. By this time, there was a strong movement for independence, and the last thing those in the movement wanted was the political entity called the Federation of Rhodesia and Nyasaland that the British imposed in 1953. Kenneth Kaunda joined Nyasaland independence leader Dr. H. Kamuzu Banda and others in protesting the federation.

In 1950, Kaunda had helped found the Lubwa branch of the African National Congress. This organization, formed in South Africa in 1912 to protest laws that deprived native Africans of the right to own land, had grown into a political independence movement. Kaunda rose through the ranks of the Lubwa branch of the ANC and became secretary-general of the party in 1953. That same year, the twenty-five-year-old Kaunda made a bicycle tour around the country, stopping frequently to play freedom songs on his guitar. The following year, he was arrested and imprisoned for two months for being in possession of political material that had been outlawed.

During his time in prison, Kaunda welcomed the opportunity to think without the distractions of work or political activity. While incarcerated, he developed the political concept he called Zambian

Humanism. Drawing heavily on the example of Mohandas K. Gandhi, who had successfully led nonviolent protests against British colonial rule in India, this philosophy emphasized the rights of common men and women and a belief in nonviolence to attain those rights. He left prison determined to live a simple life, as had Gandhi. He became a vegetarian and did all things in moderation.

In 1958, Kaunda and others broke away from the ANC to establish an independence organization that focused on Northern Rhodesia. They called it the Zambia African National Congress (ZANC) because Zambia was the name by which they wanted their independent nation known. British colonial authorities quickly banned the ZANC, and Kenneth Kaunda was arrested and imprisoned again, this time for eight months. He had suffered a bout of tuberculosis some years earlier and had a relapse while he was in prison. He overcame the disease again, however, and was fully recovered when he was released in 1960. Over the next two years, he published two books expounding on his desire for his country's liberation and his theory of Zambian Humanism, *Black Government* and *Zambia Shall Be Free*.

He immediately returned to his political work and led the reorganization of the ZANC into the United National Independence Party (UNIP), of which he was elected president. One of the major aims of the UNIP was to work with Dr. Banda's Malawi Congress Party in Nyasaland to end the federation of the two countries. In 1962 UNIP won fourteen seats in the colonial legislative assembly. Kaunda then arranged a coalition of his party with the African National Congress, and as a result he was named Minister of Local Government and Social Welfare. Two years later, the UNIP won a majority in the assembly. By this time, the British had agreed to transfer power to native Northern Rhodesians. Kenneth Kaunda was asked to form a new government. He served as prime minister of Northern Rhodesia's interim government until October 1964, when the nation achieved full independence as Zambia.

On October 24, 1964, Kaunda became the first president of the newly independent Zambia. Like other former colonies, it was a new nation with few resources, heavy debt, declining foreign aid, and a legacy of colonialism to overcome.

Kaunda's decision to focus on Zambia's copper mines as the chief source of wealth turned out to be a mistake when copper prices plummeted. Violence plagued the 1968 elections, and continued unrest caused Kaunda to ban all opposing political parties four years later. Like many other newly independent African nations, Zambia became a one-party state.

Despite his work schedule, Kaunda wrote two more books, *Letter to My Children* and *Kaunda on Violence*, both of which were widely read. But his writings had more influence than his political and economic policies. By the mid-1980s corruption and economic decline had eroded popular support for Kaunda and his party. The worst drought in Central African history, an overwhelming AIDS epidemic whose victims included his own son, and a young and discontented population who neither remembered nor cared about Kaunda's role in achieving Zambian independence were all against him. He was forced to yield to calls for multiparty elections. In 1991, he lost the presidential election to Frederick Chiluba, leader of the Movement for Multiparty Democracy (MMD).

Kaunda retired from politics for five years. When he tried to run for the presidency again in 1996, he was barred on constitutional grounds. He has since turned his attention to writing and working for AIDS causes.

PATRICE
LUMUMBA

(1925–1961)

Patrice Lumumba was born on July 2, 1925, in the Kasai Province of the Belgian African colony called Congo (loosely named after the ancient empire of Bakongo). He was a member of the Beteteta tribe, a subgroup of the Mongo people. He received his elementary education at a local missionary school but was unable to pursue further schooling and continued his education by himself through extensive reading.

As soon as he was old enough, he left home and moved to Stanleyville, named for the British reporter Henry Stanley, who became famous for finding the British explorer David Livingstone, who disappeared looking for the source of the Nile River. In Stanleyville, Lumumba got a job as a post office clerk. An avid reader of newspapers, he was also a frequent contributor of letters and articles. Unlike other Congolese writers of the time, he was less interested in the cultural heritage of his own tribe than in problems of racial, social, and economic discrimination.

On July 1, 1956, Lumumba was arrested on charges of stealing post office funds. He was convicted and sentenced to two years in prison. He appealed the sentence, which was reduced first to eighteen months and then to twelve months after he paid back the funds he was accused of stealing. On his release, Lumumba left Stanleyville and went to Leopoldville, a city named for King Leopold of Belgium. There he found work as director of sales in a beer brewery.

Lumumba began serious political activity in Leopoldville. He joined several organizations, including a social research study group that had been created in 1955. Among the more prominent members of this group was Joseph Ileo, editor in chief of a bimonthly publication called *African Conscience*. In 1956, Ileo had published a plan that called for the independence of Congo in thirty years. That same year, he had helped to establish a moderate nationalist organization called the Congolese National Movement (in French, the official language of the colony, the name was Movement Nationale Congolais, so the initials were MNC). Lumumba joined the MNC.

Lumumba quickly dominated the MNC and proclaimed himself chairman of its central committee. On October 10, 1958, he announced the formation of a national movement dedicated to the goal of liberation. Later that year, he attended the Pan-African Conference in Accra, Ghana, organized by Ghana's Prime Minister Kwame Nkrumah. Nkrumah was himself a nationalist who would later become the first president of independent Ghana. At the Accra conference, Lumumba was much influenced by Nkrumah and also became more sensitive to the notion of Pan-Africanism. The experience, in fact, radicalized him.

When he returned home, he was determined that independence would be accomplished without delay. Events seemed to be moving in that direction when Belgium announced its intention to ease Congo toward self-government. But if Belgian authorities had expected Lumumba to be grateful for this positive step, they were wrong.

Invited by a Belgian organization dedicated to the promotion of African culture to give a series of lectures in Brussels, the capital of Belgium, he insulted his hosts and sponsors by accusing non-Africans of destroying African culture. He also repeated his determination to put an end to Belgian colonization, which he likened to camouflaged slavery, and to elect an independent government by 1961. In so doing, he made powerful enemies.

As the target date for independence approached, the coalition of groups fighting for independence began to splinter. Several of Lumumba's earlier supporters withdrew from the MNC in order to form their own parties. Lumumba then had to turn his attention to rebuilding his weakened political party in time for the elections for a new government. At a party congress in late October 1959, he made statements about Belgium that the colonial authorities could not allow to go unpunished. On November 1, 1959, Lumumba was arrested for making treasonous statements and sentenced to six months in jail. Lumumba was set free only after a delegation from the MNC threatened to boycott the 1960 conference in Brussels to set forth the plan and schedule for independence.

Lumumba's party was victorious in the elections, held soon after his release, for representatives to serve in an interim government. Lumumba was elected as representative of Orientale Province and thus appointed to the General Executive College, a governing group established after the Brussels conference. But shortly after the election, his party splintered again as the vice chairman, accusing Lumumba of being too radical, left to form his own party. Lumumba reorganized the MNC yet again and in the next election gained more seats in the House of Representatives than any other party (34 of 137 seats). He then set about making alliances with the minor parties.

On June 23, 1960, Congo became officially independent as the nation of Zaire, with Lumumba as prime minister and Joseph Kasavubu as president. Lumumba was the stronger leader, but he was also more controversial. At the formal independence ceremony, he chastised Belgium for not better preparing the country for self-rule by not building more roads and hospitals and schools. The embarrassed Belgians would not forget what he had done.

Lumumba dreamed of creating a united Zaire. He also dreamed of an Africa that was completely independent of European colonial rule, and he pledged to give assistance to the African nations to the east and the south of Zaire that were struggling in their own independence movements. He was regarded by many as a leader of all Africa, not just of one nation. But he was one of the few leaders in Zaire who had such a wide perspective, and he never had a chance to put any of his ideas into action.

Most of the others in power in Zaire had dreams of controlling their own territory. Moise Tshombe, the most powerful politician in Katanga Province, did just that, with the help of Belgium, in the same month that independence was declared. Other politicians in the country were similarly concerned with their own tribal ideals and hostilities.

Outbreaks of violence caused Lumumba to ask the United Nations to send in troops to restore order. When he discovered that the UN troops were not there to do his private bidding, however, he appealed to the Soviet Union for help. That appeal sealed his fate as an enemy of the West. In that Cold War period everyone in the world was expected to side with either the communists or the capitalists.

In September 1960, President Kasavubu dismissed Prime Minister Lumumba from the government, although the new Zaire constitution gave him no authority to do so. A few days later, Kasavubu supported the overthrow of the Lumumba government by Col. Joseph Mobutu. Lumumba escaped to Port Francqui. On December 1, 1960, he was arrested by Mobutu's troops and flown to Leopoldville, where he was to be tried for inciting the army to rebellion, among other crimes.

He was treated horribly. His captors seemed to delight in beating him in front of newsreel cameras. They dragged him by a rope around his neck. Lumumba never protested. In fact, he behaved with such dignity and courage that he became a hero even to some who disagreed with his policies and actions.

Patrice Lumumba was assassinated in March 1961. For forty years, suspicions remained that powerful outside forces had been behind the people who had actually done the killing. In February 2002, the Belgian government finally admitted to a "portion of responsibility in the events that led to the death of Lumumba." In July 2002, the U.S. government released documents that revealed that the Central Intelligence Agency had also played a role in Lumumba's assassination. The CIA had supported Mobutu with money, weapons, and military training for his forces, even though the agency knew that Lumumba was a nationalist, not a communist.

Some historians believe that the death of Lumumba dealt a major setback to the southward spread of the independence movement and that if he had lived and remained in power countries like Angola would have gained independence sooner. There is no question that his death frustrated the people of Zaire in their dream of independence. The nation has had a rough time in the years since then as tribal factionalism has embroiled it in violence again and again. A long series of coups resulted in the suspension of the constitution in 1981 and the banning of political parties. A new constitution, restoring multiparty politics, was approved in 1992. Lt. Jerry Rawlings, head of state since 1981, won presidential elections in 1992 and 1996. The Republic of Zaire was renamed the Democratic Republic of the Congo in 1998.

Kofi
ANNAN
(B. 1938)

Kofi Annan was born in Kumasi in the British colony called Gold Coast (modern-day Ghana) on April 8, 1938. His father was governor of his province and also a chief in the Fante tribe. Kofi attended elementary and secondary school in Kumasi and was a track star at Mfantsipim School, an all-boys school operated by the Methodist Church. He then began his college career at the University of Science and Technology in Kumasi, where he majored in economics. Tall and strapping, he was a popular student and a natural leader. He was a track star at his own college and vice president of the Ghana Students' Union, which drew its membership from colleges around the country. It was an exciting time to be involved in student political activity, because in 1957 while Kofi Annan was in college, Gold Coast and neighboring Togoland merged into the independent state of Ghana, the first country in colonial Africa to gain its independence.

Officials of the American philanthropic organization, the Ford Foundation, had a program for providing scholarships to U.S. colleges to promising young Africans. While attending a meeting of African

student leaders in Sierra Leone, Annan was spotted by a Ford Foundation executive who was looking for bright young Africans who would benefit from an education in the United States. Annan quickly accepted the offer of a full scholarship at Macalester College, a small liberal arts college in St. Paul, Minnesota.

Leaving Africa and traveling to attend a college half a world away was a profound life change for Annan. To begin with, he had never experienced the intense cold of a Minnesota winter. When the temperatures dipped below freezing, he became accustomed to wearing winter clothes, but he did not like the way he looked in ear muffs and refused to wear them. He went out for a walk one day and nearly froze his ears. After that, he bought the biggest pair of ear muffs he could find. He later said he learned an important lesson that first winter in Minnesota: "Never walk into an environment and assume that you understand it better than the people who live there."

Annan was a member of the Macalester track team, which won a Minnesota championship meet in 1960. He was also a state champion in oratory and president of the Cosmopolitan Club, a group that promoted friendship between U.S. and international students.

Annan received his bachelor's degree in economics from Macalester in 1961. He had planned to return home to work at a new mill that the Pillsbury baking company planned to build in Ghana. But Pillsbury's plans fell through and the mill was not built. Instead of returning to Ghana, Annan went to Geneva, Switzerland, to do postgraduate work in international studies. It would prove to be a pivotal move. From then on, he would devote most of his life to international relations.

In 1962, he joined the United Nations system in the budget office of the World Health Organization (WHO), with headquarters in Sweden. The twenty-four-year-old Annan had the lowest professional designation in the international civil service. He spent three years with WHO before returning to Africa as a staffer of the UN's Economic

Commission for Africa in Addis Ababa, Ethiopia. His work dealt with development projects, such as building irrigation systems to increase farming opportunities.

In 1971, Annan went back to the United States to study for a master's degree in management at the Sloan School of Management at the Massachusetts Institute of Technology. He earned his degree in 1972 and two years later returned to Ghana as Director of the Ghana Tourist Development Company. He believed that the tourism business had great economic potential for his homeland, and with the skills he had acquired through his various jobs and his studies, he was excited about helping his country.

But it was hard to build a tourism industry in a country that was so politically unstable. Ethnic and tribal conflicts, economic problems, and a host of other issues seemed guaranteed to prevent Ghana from enjoying a stable government. A long series of coups, or takeovers of the government by the military, put a damper on Annan's plans to help his country. He realized he could not build tourism until there was peace.

Annan returned to the United Nations. He spent more than a decade at different posts, which included the United Nations Emergency Force (UNEF II) in Ismailia, Egypt, and the Office of the United Nations High Commissioner for Refugees (UNHCR) in Geneva, Switzerland. He met and married Nane Lagergren, a Swedish artist and lawyer. Her uncle, the Swedish diplomat Raoul Wallenberg, had helped thousands of Hungarian Jews escape from the Nazis during World War II.

In 1987, Annan joined United Nations headquarters in New York City as Assistant Secretary-General for Human Resources Management and Security Coordinator for the UN System. He spent three years in that position before becoming Assistant Secretary-General for Program Planning, Budget and Finance, and he became Controller in 1990.

He was then appointed Assistant Secretary-General for Peacekeeping Operations. One of his first duties brought him international recognition. During the Persian Gulf War, he negotiated the release of UN staff in Iraq. After a year, he was promoted to Undersecretary-General. During his three years in this office, the United Nations' peacekeeping operation grew to an enormous size and scope. Ethnic conflict in Bosnia and Herzegovina, the former Yugoslavia, threatened the stability of that entire region, and the majority of member nations of the UN determined to keep the peace. A force of almost seventy thousand military and civilian personnel from seventy-seven countries was deployed to the region. Kofi Annan was in charge of the entire effort. He helped to negotiate the Dayton Peace Agreement that ended the war, and then served as Special Representative of the Secretary-General of the United Nations, overseeing the transition to peacetime peacekeeping operations under the North Atlantic Treaty Organization.

The Secretary-General of the United Nations at the time was Boutros Boutros-Ghali of Egypt. When in late 1996, Boutros-Ghali came up for a second term, the United States vetoed his reelection. Boutros-Ghali had been the first UN Secretary-General from Africa, and the UN Security Council, which elects the Secretary-General, realized it was still Africa's "turn." Both the United States and France backed the election of Kofi Annan, and on January 1, 1997, he became the seventh Secretary-General of the United Nations. He was also the first black African to hold the highest office of the world body and the first to have come up through the ranks of the UN.

Because he had been backed by the United States, some observers expected Annan to side with the United States on matters that came before the United Nations. But he proved to be independent—even in the face of strong pressure. Often hampered by the UN's financial crisis, he nevertheless learned to do much with little and was determined to reassert the central role of the United Nations in global relations.

His priorities as Secretary-General have been to revitalize the United Nations through a comprehensive program of reform; to strengthen the organization's traditional work in the areas of development and the maintenance of international peace and security; to encourage and advocate human rights, the rule of law, and the universal values of equality, tolerance, and human dignity found in the United Nations Charter; and to increase respect and restore public confidence in the organization by reaching out to new partners and, in his words, by "bringing the United Nations closer to the people."

In April 2000, he issued a Millennium Report titled "We the Peoples: The Role of the United Nations in the 21st Century," calling on member states to commit themselves to an action plan for ending poverty and inequality, improving education, reducing HIV/AIDS, safeguarding the environment, and protecting people from deadly conflict and violence.

In April 2001, he issued a five-point "Call to Action" to address the HIV/AIDS epidemic, which he described as his personal priority, and proposed the establishment of a Global AIDS and Health Fund to serve as a mechanism for some of the increased spending needed to help developing countries confront the crisis.

In June 2001, the United Nations General Assembly appointed him by acclamation to a second term of office, beginning on January 1, 2002, and ending on December 31, 2006. Six months later, on December 10, 2001, Kofi Annan as Secretary-General and the United Nations as a body were awarded the Nobel Peace Prize. In awarding the prize to Annan, the Nobel Committee credited him with having been "preeminent in bringing new life to the organization." In also conferring the prize to the United Nations, the committee said it wished "to proclaim that the only negotiable road to global peace and cooperation goes by way of the United Nations."

STEPHEN
BIKO
(1946–1977)

Like Patrice Lumumba, Stephen Biko was a martyr to the cause of African nationalism. Unlike Lumumba, however, Biko never sought political office or dreamed of running a nation. He was a committed activist for black nationalism and against apartheid, the system of racial separation in the country that was the last white stronghold on the African continent, South Africa. He was murdered by South African authorities because of his work.

Stephen Biko was born in the Eastern Cape Province of South Africa, one of four children of Mathew Mzingaye Biko and Alice Nokuzola Biko. Two years after his birth, the National Party took control of the government of South Africa. Members in the National Party were primarily Afrikaaners, descendants of the nineteenth-century Dutch settlers in South Africa. Once in control, the National Party government of Prime Minister Ian Smith instituted a nationwide policy of apartheid, or strict separation of the races. When Great Britain protested this policy, South Africa left the British Commonwealth of Nations.

Young Steve Biko had little awareness of these outside events as he completed his elementary and secondary schooling. He was an able student who skipped a grade in elementary school and so outdistanced his classmates in his studies that when he was in high school he volunteered to teach his classmates in the evenings.

In 1963, at the age of seventeen, he was admitted to Lovedale College, but he was not to be there long. His older brother, Khaya Biko, had joined the Pan-Africanist Congress. The PAC had been formed in 1959 as a breakaway group from the African National Congress. Like the ANC, it was an African nationalist organization that vowed to fight colonialism and apartheid. Khaya Biko had tried to persuade Steve to join the PAC as well, and Steve had attended a few meetings. That was enough to get him expelled from Lovedale. This expulsion marked a turning point in the younger man's life.

Biko was able to continue his schooling. In 1964, he enrolled at St. Francis College, where he concentrated on his studies. But all the while he was thinking and reading and forming his own ideas about freedom. Two years later he was admitted to the Medical School of Natal University in the city of Durban, and as soon as he arrived on the campus of the medical school he became politically active. He joined the National Union of South African Students (NUSAS), an interracial group, and attended two annual conferences of the group at Rhodes University in 1966 and 1967.

After a time, however, he became convinced that the interests of the white students and the black students were too dissimilar to make the NUSAS worthwhile—at least for him. In particular, he felt that the white students didn't care enough about the conditions under which South African blacks lived. In 1969 he broke away from the NUSAS to form the South African Students Organization (SASO). Serving as its first president, he worked tirelessly to establish branches on other college campuses and to build its membership and influence. By 1971 there were SASO branches at most universities and colleges.

Seeking to expand its influence further, in 1972 Biko formed the Black People's Convention, a national umbrella group of all the black-consciousness organizations in the country. The BPC brought together about seventy different groups and associations, such as the South African Student's Movement (SASM), the National Association of Youth Organizations (NAYO), and the Black Workers Project (BWP), which supported black workers whose unions were not recognized under the apartheid regime. Elected as the first president of the BPC, Biko was almost immediately expelled from medical school.

Biko got a job with the Black Community Program (BCP) in Durban, which he had also helped to establish. Its aim was to assist local people in helping themselves by organizing to work together. But Biko was not to be with the BCP long. By that time, South African authorities were beginning to worry about Biko's growing influence. In 1973, the government took action, banning Biko and six other black student leaders from further political action. Under the ban, Biko was restricted to his hometown in the Eastern Cape. Communications were quite primitive, and this restriction meant that he was unable to continue his political organizing on a large scale.

Instead, he organized on a small scale. He formed a number of local organizations based on the notion of self-help, including a community clinic, an organization to help support ex-political prisoners and their families, an education fund, and a leatherworks project. All of these efforts were successful, and the area became a showcase for community development.

In the meantime, Biko quietly continued his black-consciousness activity, although he was closely watched by authorities. In fact, from 1975 to 1977 he was detained and questioned three times by Eastern Cape police, who had the authority to do so under anti-terrorism laws. Biko, however, was undaunted by this official harassment. In the summer of 1977, he determined to make a second attempt to bring together the various black-consciousness and antiapartheid organizations, among them the African National Congress, the Pan-Africanist Congress, and the Black Consciousness Movement. He had been at meetings in Cape Town and had just left that city when he was arrested for a fourth time on August 18, 1977.

Taken to Port Elizabeth, he was first questioned at the regular police station. Then, on September 7, he was transferred for further interrogation to the headquarters of the security police. A common part of "interrogation" by South African police and security officers was beating, and it is likely that Biko had already been beaten extensively by the time he reached security headquarters. But there he was beaten about the head so severely that he was clearly disoriented. For two days he was chained to a metal gate, naked and in a standing position, slipping in and out of unconsciousness, while the officers waited to see if they could continue the interrogation. Doctors summoned to examine him did not recommend that he be hospitalized. Four days later, after he had slipped into a coma, they advised that he be moved to a hospital. Still naked, his body was loaded into the back of a Land Rover and transported on a twelve-hour journey over rocky roads to Pretoria, the capital of South Africa. There he was taken not to a hospital but to a cell in Pretoria Central Prison. He died there on September 12 without ever having regained consciousness.

The South African Minister of Justice initially reported that Biko had died from the effects of a hunger strike. Local and international media pressure, especially from Donald Woods, editor of the *East London Daily Dispatch* and a friend of Biko, soon caused the authorities to drop that lie. An inquest, held after intense outside pressure, revealed that Biko had died of brain damage, but the presiding magistrate failed to hold anyone responsible, ruling that the death had occurred as the result of a scuffle between Biko and the police.

This ruling set off a round of protests by black-consciousness organizations in South Africa, with the result that the government banned several organizations and leaders, including the journalist Donald

Woods. Under continued international pressure, the United Nations Security Council took action against South Africa by banning sales of arms to the country.

Over the next decade, South Africa became more and more isolated from the rest of the world, as international sports organizations refused to allow South African teams to compete, international businesses stopped doing business with South Africa, and individuals and businesses stopped investing in South African businesses. By the mid 1980s, a combination of international pressure and agitation on the part of African political and labor groups had finally caused the tide to turn against apartheid. In 1985, in a second inquiry into Biko's death, the doctors who failed to recommend immediate hospitalization were censured. But not until apartheid ended and a new, black-majority government headed by the South African hero Nelson Mandela was in place, did the truth about the death of Steve Biko come out. The Mandela government set up the Truth and Reconciliation Commission, which opened hearings into the human rights abuses committed during the apartheid years. People who testified before the commission were promised amnesty, or immunity from prosecution, provided that they told the commission the full truth about their crimes and could prove a political motive. The widow of Steve Biko and the families of two other victims filed a lawsuit challenging the commission's power to grant amnesty to perpetrators in exchange for the truth, but they were unsuccessful.

The police officers responsible for Biko's death applied for amnesty to the Truth and Reconciliation Commission, which found that his death in detention had been a gross violation of human rights and denied them amnesty. This decision opened the way for prosecution of the officers in the courts. In the fall of 2003, Justice Ministry officials announced that the officers would not be prosecuted. Because the killing had taken place twenty-five years earlier, the statute of limitations for prosecution on charges of assault and homicide had expired.

But the main reason was insufficient evidence, for there had been no witnesses to the beating except the five officers themselves.

The African National Congress and Biko's family criticized the ruling. A government spokesman gave assurances that if new evidence came to light at a later date, the case could be reopened.

It will be many decades before the problems of Africa are resolved, the bitter legacy of apartheid and European colonialism overcome, the tribal rivalries ended. New heroes will arise who will lead their separate nations and the continent as a whole to peace and prosperity. The developed nations of the world, who benefited from Africa's human and natural resources for so long, can help speed the process by supporting those heroes of the future and helping make the nations of Africa truly independent and self-sustaining.

FURTHER READING

BOOKS

Ayo, Yvonne. *Africa*. New York: Alfred A. Knopf, 1995.

Chambers, Catherine. *West African States: 15th Century to Colonial Era.* Austin: Raintree Steck-Vaughn, 1999.

Courlander, Harold, comp. *The Crest and the Hide: And Other African Stories of Heroes, Chiefs, Bards, Hunters, Sorcerers, and Common People.* New York: Coward, McCann & Geoghegan, 1982.

Haskins, James, and Kathleen Benson. *African Beginnings.* New York: Lothrop, Lee & Shepard Books, 1998.

Haskins, Jim. *Count Your Way through Africa.* Minneapolis: Carolrhoda Books, 1992.

Haskins, Jim, and Joann Biondi. *From Afar to Zulu: A Dictionary of African Cultures.* New York: Walker and Company, 1995.

Mathabane, Mark A. *Kaffir Boy: The True Story of a Black Youth Coming of Age in South Africa.* New York: Touchstone Books, 1998.

Rogers, J. A., John Henrik Clarke, editors. *World's Great Men of Color.* Vol. I. Reprint, New York: Touchstone Books, 1996.

INTERNET RESOURCES

The Story of Africa: BBC World Service
www.bbc.co.uk/worldservice/africa/features/storyofafrica/index.shtml

Africa: One Continent. Many Worlds.
A collaborative project of the Field Museum, Chicago, the Natural History Museum of Los Angeles County, the California African American Museum, Los Angeles, and the Armory Center for the Arts, Pasadena, California.
www.nhm.org/africa/

Picture Credits

Page 8: Statuette of Imhotep (reproduction), Ptolemaic Period, 330–23 BC, bronze, 11.7 x 4 cm, The Art Institute of Chicago, gift of Henry H. Getty, Charles L. Hutchinson, Robert H. Fleming, and Norman W. Harris, 1892.160, photo by Bob Hashimoto; page 11: P. 3003/N. 2073 EGYPT, Gebel Barkal (Napata) Altar of Piye (Piyankhy), side chapel, Great Temple of Amon; page 15: © Nik Wheeler/Corbis; page 20: Bibliothèque nationale de France; page 24: Tomb of Askia Mohamed, Gao, Mali, photo by Marli Shamir, c. 1969; page 31: The John Carter Brown Library, Brown University, Providence, R.I.; page 35: courtesy of G. F. Kojo Arthur and CEFIKS Publications, Beltsville, Md.; pages 45 and 49: © Hulton-Deutsch Collection/Corbis; page 51: courtesy of Ray Justin Hoole; page 56: Getty Images; page 60: © Stapleton Collection/Corbis; page 64: Getty Images; pages 69, 76: © Hulton-Deutsch Collection/Corbis; page 81: © Genevieve Chauvel/Sygma/Corbis; page 83: Getty Images; pages 86, 89: © Bettmann/Corbis; pages 94, 99: Getty Images; page 106: © Jacquest M. Chenet/Corbis; page 113: © Peter Turnley/Corbis; page 115: © Time Life Pictures/Getty Images; pages 122, 125: © Hulton-Deutsch Collection/Corbis; page 129: © Bettmann/Corbis; page 134: © Time Life Pictures/Getty Images; page 139: © Keystone/Getty Images; page 145: © Najlah Feanny/Corbis; page 151: AP/Wide World Photos.

INDEX